The Non-Aligned World

The Non-Aligned World

Striking Out in an Era of Great Power Competition

JORGE HEINE,
CARLOS FORTIN AND
CARLOS OMINAMI

polity

First published in 2025 by Polity Press

Polity Press
65 Bridge Street
Cambridge CB2 1UR, UK

Polity Press
111 River Street
Hoboken, NJ 07030, USA

ISBN-13: 978-1-5095-6434-7
ISBN-13: 978-1-5095-6435-4 (pb)

A catalogue record for this book is available from the British Library.

Library of Congress Control Number: 2024947184

Typeset in 11 on 13 pt Sabon
by Cheshire Typesetting Ltd, Cuddington, Cheshire
Printed and bound in Great Britain by TJ Books Ltd, Padstow, Cornwall

For further information on Polity, visit our website:
politybooks.com

Dedicated to the memory of Celso Furtado, Aníbal Pinto and Raúl Prebisch, brilliant economists and far-sighted thinkers, whose path-breaking work foresaw the rise of the South.

Contents

Figures and Tables

Figures

Tables

Acknowledgments

In the course of the five years since we first put forward the notion of Active Non-Alignment, we have accumulated significant debts to various entities and colleagues that have believed in this project and have supported it in various ways, mainly by hosting meetings to discuss its implications. They include the Foro Permanente de Política Exterior in Santiago; the Institute of International Studies of the University of Chile; the Chile 21 Foundation; FLACSO-Chile and FLACSO-Argentina; the School of International Relations at the Getulio Vargas Foundation in São Paulo; the School of Public Policy at the University of British Columbia in Vancouver; the Elliott School of International Affairs at George Washington University in Washington DC; the School of International Studies at Jawaharlal Nehru University in New Delhi; the South African Institute of International Affairs (SAIIA) in Johannesburg; the Fulbright Association of New Jersey; the Sir Arthur Lewis Institute of Social and Economic Studies (ISER) at the University of the West Indies in Mona, Jamaica; the Institute of International Relations (IIR) of the University of the West Indies, St. Augustine, in Trinidad and Tobago; Ashoka University in New Delhi; the Columbus Memorial

Library at the Organization of American States (OAS) in Washington DC; the Maison de l'Amérique Latine in Paris; La Maison Française at New York University (NYU); the Global Development Policy Center at Boston University; the Instituto Matías Romero of the Mexican Foreign Ministry in Mexico City; the journal *Global Policy*; the French journal *Le Grand Continent*; the Canadian Association for Latin American and Caribbean Studies; the Latin American Studies Association (LASA); and the International Political Science Association (IPSA). A special thanks to Eva-Maria Nag and Gregory Chin of the *Global Policy* journal for their unwavering support.

Much as this project has been a collaborative endeavor between the three of us, we are also in debt to colleagues who have generously shared their views of earlier versions of the text, allowing us to refine and sharpen our argument: they include Jorge Dominguez, Bernabe Malacalza and Matias Spektor; Gregory Chin and Trita Parsi provided valuable feedback on Chapter 2, and Kishore Mahbubani did so on Chapter 5. We are also indebted to two anonymous readers engaged by Polity Press for their very valuable comments and suggestions. Any shortcomings in the text are our fault alone. As with several of our previous books, our long-time collaborator, Dr. Joseph Turcotte, with his remarkable editing skills, has played a key role in giving proper shape to what was at one point a somewhat unwieldy manuscript.

Finally, we would like to thank that extraordinary editor that is Louise Knight at Polity Press for believing in this project from the word go and for shepherding it so effectively through its various stages.

August 2024
Jorge Heine, Boston, Massachusetts
Carlos Fortin, Brighton, England
Carlos Ominami, Paris, France

Abbreviations

ADMM+	ASEAN Defense Ministers' Meeting Plus
AIIB	Asian Investment and Infrastructure Bank
AMLO	President Andrés Manuel López Obrador (Mexico)
ANA	Active Non-Alignment
AOIP	ASEAN Outlook on the Indo-Pacific
APEC	Asia-Pacific Economic Cooperation
APEP	Americas Partnership for Economic Prosperity
ARF	ASEAN Regional Forum
ASEAN	Association of Southeast Asian Nations
ASEAN + 3	ASEAN plus China, Japan and South Korea
BRI	Belt and Road Initiative
BRIC	Brazil, Russia, India and China
BRICS	BRIC plus South Africa
BRICS+	Expansion of the BRICS group
CARICOM	Caribbean Community
CCP	Chinese Communist Party
CELAC	Community of Latin American and Caribbean States
CIS	Community of Independent States

CPSU	Communist Party of the Soviet Union
CPTPP	Comprehensive and Progressive Agreement for Trans-Pacific Partnership
EAS	East Asia Summit
ECFR	European Council on Foreign Relations
ECLAC	Economic Commission for Latin America and the Caribbean
ECOSOC	United Nations Economic and Social Council
EU	European Union
EV	electric vehicle
FDI	foreign direct investment
FOIP	Free and Open Indo-Pacific
FTA	free trade agreement
FTAA	Free Trade Area of the Americas
G7	Group of 7
G20	Group of 20
G77+China	Group of 77
GATT	General Agreement on Tariffs and Trade
GDP	gross domestic product
IBSA	India, Brazil and South Africa
ICC	International Criminal Court
ICJ	International Court of Justice
ICSID	International Center for the Settlement of Investment Disputes (World Bank)
IDFC	International Development Finance Corporation
IFI	international financial institution
IIR	Institute of International Relations (University of the West Indies, St. Augustine)
IMF	International Monetary Fund
IP	intellectual property
IPSA	International Political Science Association
IR	international relations
IRA	Inflation Reduction Act (United States)

ISDS	investor-state dispute settlement
ISER	Sir Arthur Lewis Institute of Social and Economic Studies (University of the West Indies, Mona)
LAC	Latin America and the Caribbean
LASA	Latin American Studies Association
LIO	liberal international order
MDGs	Millenium Development Goals
MERCOSUR	Southern Common Market
MOU	Memorandum of Understanding
NAM	Non-Aligned Movement
NATO	North Atlantic Treaty Organization
NDB	New Development Bank, so-called BRICS Bank
NDRC	National Development and Reform Commission
NGO	non-governmental organization
NIEO	New International Economic Order
OAS	Organization of American States
OECD	Organisation for Economic Co-operation and Development
P-5	Permanent 5
PPP	purchasing power parity
R&D	research and development
RBO	rules-based order
RCEP	Regional Comprehensive Economic Partnership
RMB	renminbi
SAIIA	South African Institute of International Affairs
SCO	Shanghai Cooperation Organization
SDR	IMF Special Drawing Rights
SEANWFZ	Southeast Asia Nuclear Weapon Free Zone
SOA	Summit of the Americas
SOE	state-owned enterprise

TAC	Treaty of Amity and Cooperation in Southeast Asia
TPP	Trans-Pacific Partnership
UAE	United Arab Emirates
UN	United Nations
UNASUR	Union of South American Nations
UNCTAD	United Nations Conference on Trade and Development
UNDP	United Nations Development Programme
UNGA	United Nations General Assembly
UNHRC	United Nations Human Rights Council
UNSC	United Nations Security Council
USD	US dollars
WTO	World Trade Organization
XUAR	Xinjiang Uyghur Autonomous Region of China
ZOPFAN	Zone of Peace, Freedom and Neutrality

Preface

In May 2024, at a White House press conference held during a state visit to the United States, Kenyan president William Ruto was asked whether Kenya preferred Chinese or US investment. His response was: "We are facing neither East nor West. We are facing forward." In doing so, he was citing Kwame Nkrumah – Ghana's first Prime Minister and one of the founding fathers of the Non-Aligned Movement (NAM).[1]

Five years ago, we put forward the concept of Active Non-Alignment (ANA) as the best way for Latin America to deal with the crisis it faced at the time, one aggravated by the pressures it was being subjected to both by Washington and Beijing to follow their dictates.[2] The concept resonated and triggered considerable interest across the region. It was also criticized by some as anachronistic, as nothing more than an exercise in nostalgia that bore no relevance to the realities of the new century. Yet, today, non-alignment is back with a vengeance, and not just in Latin America, but also in Africa and Asia, albeit in a new incarnation, as ANA.

What is Active Non-Alignment? ANA is a foreign policy doctrine based on refusing to take sides in the Great Power competition that is a signature feature of the international system of the third decade of the new century. Deployed by developing nations that find themselves pressured by the United States, on the one hand, and by China, on the other, it puts the national interest of the country front and center – as opposed to doing so with the geopolitical concerns of others. It examines each foreign policy issue on its merits, rejecting what it considers an artificial binary choice between Washington and Beijing. The *grand strategy* of ANA is what has been called "playing the field," that is, taking advantage of this competition among the Great Powers to maximize the development opportunities for Global South nations, in a way that was not possible during the "unipolar moment" of unbridled US primacy, or even during the Cold War.

In turn, the *tactic* of ANA is that of hedging, that is, taking on a middle position between balancing and bandwagoning, while keeping options open. ANA aims to keep good relations with both (or more) Great Powers in conflict, while diversifying links as much as possible. Hedging is the best approach to deal with situations of uncertainty, in which outcomes are not assured and the downside to making the wrong choice can be devastating. A key feature of it is its *proactive* nature, always in search of new opportunities to enhance the economic growth and development of nations whose populations are badly in need of both. Ultimately, ANA aims at enhancing and strengthening national autonomy.

How does ANA differ from traditional non-alignment, i.e., the notions espoused by the NAM in its heyday?

In terms of the international setting developing nations find themselves in, there are obvious parallels between the Cold War and the current Great Power competition. In both cases, the US is pitted against a power that defines itself as Communist, and, in both cases, these parties reach out to the hearts and minds of the peoples of what used to be called the Third World and is now known as the Global South. In this context, the key principles espoused by the NAM, like those of non-intervention, peaceful coexistence, multilateralism and the respect of international law, retain their currency. The fact that we still live in the nuclear age, and the specter of nuclear annihilation has by no means disappeared, makes championing the cause of peace as dear to the ANA as it was to the NAM. That said, there are obvious differences between the two situations.

In the third decade of the new century, the geo-economic axis has shifted from the North Atlantic to the Asia Pacific.[3] Of the top ten cities with the largest number of billionaires in 2024, six are in Asia.[4] New international financial institutions (IFIs), like the Asian Investment and Infrastructure Bank (AIIB) and the New Development Bank (NDB), dot the multilateral development banking landscape. This allows for the "collective financial statecraft" of today's Global South, and the possibility of it tapping into the vast resources of projects like China's Belt and Road Initiative (BRI), amounting to a cool one trillion dollars in its first decade. This is very different from the *diplomatie des cahiers des doleances* (victimhood diplomacy) of yesterday's Third World, whose demands for vast transfers of wealth from North to South fell on deaf ears. Today's Global South thus speaks from a position of relative strength, as opposed to the considerable weakness of the Third World of the 1950s and 1960s, giving ANA much more leverage to pursue its objectives. Whereas the key platforms of non-alignment were the NAM itself and the G77 – huge, unwieldy bodies that had the power of numbers, but little else – today's ANA relies on smaller but more effective bodies, like the BRICS, that command not just ideational but also considerable material resources to attain their objectives. This signals a decisive shift in the traditionally fraught relationship between the Global North and the Global South.

Over the past five years we have continued to develop and refine the concept of ANA, which has come to the fore at a time of momentous change in world politics. A veritable cascade of earth-shattering developments – the COVID-19 pandemic; the Russian invasion of Ukraine; the dramatic expansion of the BRICS group (now known as BRICS+), representing a considerable challenge to the West; and Israel's war in Gaza in the wake of Hamas's attack on Israel – have impelled this seismic moment.

This overlapping succession of events has led some to speak of a "polycrisis,"[5] leading us to Italian philosopher Antonio Gramsci's dictum in his *Prison Notebooks* that "the crisis consists precisely in the fact that the old is dying and the new cannot be born: in this interregnum a great variety of morbid symptoms appear."[6]

What is dying is the old world order that followed the end of the Cold War in 1989–91, with the fall of the Berlin Wall and the collapse of the Soviet Union. This was a world order that, for want of a better term, came to be known as "the unipolar moment," to signify the undisputed hegemony of the US. What is not yet born is the new order that will replace it. While some refer to it as a multipolar order, others, like Amitav Acharya, speak of a multiplex order.[7] And in this transition, with the old rules falling by the wayside and the new ones not yet in place, a bit of a "free for all" persists. Thus, the seemingly chaotic state of the world today.

Yet, two phenomena stand out at this significant turning point in world affairs. One is the rise of the Global South as a force to be reckoned with in international politics. The other is the re-emergence of non-alignment as an approach to foreign policy in the post-colonial world. The two are closely associated. As key countries from the Global South contend with the many challenges of this troubled world, the conduct of their foreign policy is increasingly driven by ANA.

ANA as the way forward

So, what is ANA all about and why has it spread like wildfire?

Building on our work on the subject over the past five years, our argument in this book is the following:

(1) The world order is undergoing a major moment of transition, in many ways as significant as the one that took place at the end of the Cold War.

(2) This transition is driven by the relative decline of the hitherto-hegemonic power, the United States, and by the rapid rise of China – though also by the emergence of other rising powers, what Fareed Zakaria has referred to as "The Rise of the Rest."[8]

(3) As tends to happen in history, this dynamic has triggered a fierce Great Power competition – between Washington and Beijing. This has escalated from a trade war to a tech war to a conflict with increasingly ideological and military overtones.

(4) In this competition, weaker states, especially those in the developing world, find themselves between a rock and a hard place. In such circumstances, ANA represents the best alternative to deal with this predicament.

(5) ANA means that countries put their own national interest front and center, refusing to budge to pressure from the Great Powers. For the ANA doctrine, the grand strategy is what Kassab has called "playing the field," that is, picking and choosing among the various issues, as opposed to siding automatically with one or another of the Great Powers.[9]

(6) In turn, in terms of foreign policy tactics, ANA relies on hedging, that is, a middle position between balancing and bandwagoning, which allows states to keep their options open. This is the safest way to deal with situations of high uncertainty, such as the one the world finds itself in today, in which (once again) the specter of nuclear war has raised its ugly head.

(7) The major wars that arose in 2022–4 – mainly the war in Ukraine resulting from Russia's invasion, and Israel's war on Gaza after being attacked by Hamas – have brought to the fore the growing rift between North and South.

(8) Yet, far from being fundamental causes of this rift, these wars and the reactions to them in the South are expressions of a much deeper malaise of the post-colonial world with current international arrangements.

(9) Thus, the rise of the Global South reflects the view in Africa, Asia and Latin America that the Great Powers today do little to deal with global issues like climate change, pandemics and the rise of international organized crime, or with the pressing concerns of developing nations such as financial indebtedness, food and water scarcity and mass migrations. Instead, the Great Powers seem more focused on petty squabbles among themselves, on issues like erecting artificial islands in the South China Sea, or raising prohibitive tariffs on electric vehicles (EVs) in each other's markets, instead of dealing with the world's very real major problems. Simply by working together on these issues, the US and China, which together represent 40 percent of the world's gross domestic product (GDP), could do much to resolve them, if only they set their minds to it.

(10) In this context, ANA emerges as a powerful tool and guide to action in an uncertain world. If deftly handled, it can do much to enhance the development opportunities for what is increasingly referred to as the Global Majority.

1

The War in Ukraine: Reactions from the Global South

The war in Ukraine triggered by Russia's invasion on February 24, 2022, constitutes the most significant *casus belli* in Europe since the end of World War II.[1] As of this writing, two-and-a-half years after the war began, it shows no sign of coming to an end. The 8 million refugees, and the hundreds of thousands of fatalities, civilian and military, that the war has caused are proof positive of how wrongheaded the notions proclaiming Europe as a continent of peace had been. Those notions – based on the idea that Europe had left behind the nationalisms of yore; that it had learned the lessons of the tragic first half of the twentieth century; and that it was embarked upon building a regional space in which nation-states and national borders would be relegated to a distant past, thus bringing about a permanent *Pax Europaea* – have been shown to be misguided.[2] The images of modern apartment buildings destroyed by missiles and bombs of various kinds, and of old ladies fleeing, with a few belongings in hand, from their ancestral villages, now razed to the ground, cannot but shock us deeply.

German Chancellor Olaf Scholz, as the leader of Europe's largest economy, has played a key role in the European Union's reaction to the war. And it was he who, drawing on the extraordinary ability of the German language to coin new terms by merely pasting words together, coined the one that perhaps best defines the meaning of this tragic war: *Zeitenwende*,[3] that is, a change of epoch. Scholz was referring not just to the war itself, but to the end of an era in which Germany's industrial development benefited from access to cheap and plentiful Russian oil and gas. In 2023, Germany, which is not formally involved in the war in Ukraine, had lower economic growth than Russia – a country that is not only a party in the war, but also suffers the devastating consequences of Western economic and financial sanctions that have effectively excluded the country from the international banking system and frozen $300 billion (USD) in Russian assets abroad.[4]

There is no doubt that the Russian invasion of Ukraine was an open violation of international law and of the United Nations Charter. Respect of national sovereignty has been a bedrock principle of the international system. This was crassly ignored on February 24, 2022, as was the principle of non-intervention in the affairs of other states. According to the 1991 Minsk Treaty among the Commonwealth of Independent States (CIS), that is, the former (now independent) Soviet republics, Ukraine would proceed to dismantle the nuclear weapons it had inherited from the former Soviet Union, and deliver them to its successor state, the Russian Federation. In turn, according to the 1994 Budapest Memorandum, Russia committed to guarantee the security of Ukraine in case of an attack on it – which in this case was undertaken by Russia itself.[5]

It should thus not be surprising that the reaction of many countries across the world was an immediate condemnation of Russia's invasion. For obvious reasons, this was especially so in Europe and in North America, that is, across the North Atlantic and especially in North Atlantic Treaty Organization (NATO) member states. Paradoxically, Moscow's action ended up being a boon to NATO. The alliance, which had been previously affected by strong divisions, particularly during the years of the first Trump administration, closed ranks as it had seldom done before. Countries that until then had kept out of NATO, like Finland and Sweden, changed their minds and joined it, strengthening the alliance and completing a front that would cover almost the whole Western border of the Russian Federation.

Given that the Russian justification for invading Ukraine was to stop NATO's Eastern expansion (which NATO undertook not just by incorporating former Soviet allies in the Warsaw Pact, but also by opening the door to former Soviet provinces like Ukraine and Georgia), this is ironic.[6] It is, in many ways, a classic case of a self-fulfilling prophecy.[7]

The reaction of the Global South

Beyond this "boomerang effect" of Russia's "special operation" (in Moscow's euphemism) in Ukraine on NATO, the European Union (EU) and the Group of Seven, and the new sense of purpose with which this imbued the Western alliance, what was the reaction to it in the rest of the world, i.e., in Africa, Asia and Latin America?

From many young and mostly small countries – most of which came into independence only after World War II and have a deep attachment to their newly acquired sovereignty and to the principle of non-intervention in international affairs – one might have expected a reaction like that of Western nations. The unprovoked attack on Ukraine could well be seen as a classic case of a Great Power bullying a smaller state, a crass attempt to subject it to its own will, if not downright annex it, as Russia had done previously with Crimea in 2014.

This could well have been seen as the ultimate nightmare for developing nations, a precedent-setting breaking of the established rules of the existing international order, something that tomorrow could happen to any other country.

And yes, most of the United Nations (UN) member states condemned the Russian invasion, some 142 (out of 193) in a UN General Assembly vote on March 1, 2022. But the vote was far from unanimous. Some of the largest countries in the world, like India, China, Pakistan and South Africa, refused to condemn the invasion, and further resolutions in April of that year, designed to punish Russia for its actions (like the one suspending its membership in the UN Human Rights Council [UNHRC]), garnered fewer votes and elicited some pushback.

In that regard, the case of Latin America is especially revealing. In a region with a strong tradition of commitment to international law, whose nations represented 40 percent of the founding membership of the UN, and that for historical reasons has always stood up for the principle of non-intervention in international affairs, one could have expected a closing of ranks with the West's position on the war in Ukraine. The close association in defense and security matters with the US, and the often-mentioned cultural affinity of many South American countries, especially those of the Southern Cone, with Europe, led many to assume that this closing of ranks would occur. But, although the overall reaction was mixed, and with many gradations, it did not happen that way.

No Latin American country voted against the UN General Assembly (UNGA) resolution of March 1, 2022, condemning the Russian invasion; four (Bolivia, Cuba, El Salvador and Nicaragua) abstained, and one (Venezuela) did not vote. However, things changed when it came to the resolution on suspending Russia from the UNHRC, which several Latin American countries opposed. And there was also the curious phenomenon of a gap between what we might call presidential diplomacy (diplomacy led by the head of state) and that conducted by the foreign ministries.

In two of the region's biggest countries, Argentina and Mexico, which often lead the way in Latin America's relations with the rest of the world, this became especially apparent.[8]

While the presidents expressed their refusal to take sides on the issue of the war, their foreign ministries took positions much closer to Washington's. In the case of Mexico, this was taken to the limit by President Andrés Manuel López Obrador, popularly known as AMLO, who quickly drifted away from his initial stance of condemning the invasion, while Mexico's mission to the UN in New York coordinated positions with the US on the drafting of resolutions that did precisely that. Two other Latin American presidents, Jair Bolsonaro of Brazil and Alberto Fernández of Argentina, had undertaken state visits to Russia in February 2022, shortly before the start of the war, with Bolsonaro stating that he was in Moscow "in solidarity with Russia."[9] Latin America's rejection of the Western stance on the Ukraine war came to a head when both the US and Germany, in a request undergirded by an official visit by Olaf Scholz to Argentina, Brazil and Chile in January 2023, formally asked several Latin American countries to provide weapons to Ukraine, a request that was publicly rejected by all the countries involved.

If this was the case in Latin America, in Africa the refusal to stand with the West on the issue of the war in Ukraine was even more pronounced. At the March 1 UNGA vote, "Africa was split down the middle, with 27 states voting for the resolution, one voting against it (Eritrea), and the rest abstaining or absent from the vote."[10] South Africa, which abstained, took an especially vocal stance, arguing that the resolution would only make matters worse. In the UNGA vote to suspend Russia from the UNHRC, only ten African countries voted in favor of it, nine voted against it, twenty-three abstained and eight were not present. As South African Foreign Minister Naledi Pandor put it in a May 12, 2022 speech:

> South Africa, along with other members of the Global South, resist "becoming embroiled in the politics of confrontation and aggression that has been advocated by the powerful countries,"

> are seeking to "assert their independent, non-aligned views" and wish to promote "peaceful resolution of the conflict through dialogue and negotiation" in keeping with the approach of the Non-Aligned Movement that recognizes the right of maintaining independent foreign policies.[11]

In Southeast Asia, the reaction to the Russian invasion of Ukraine was also mixed. On March 1, 2022, eight of the ten Association of Southeast Asian Nations (ASEAN) member states voted to condemn Russia's actions, the only exceptions being Laos and Vietnam. On the April 2022 resolution to suspend Russia from the UNHRC, however, six ASEAN members abstained, Laos and Vietnam voted against it, and only the Philippines and the Myanmar government-in-exile voted in favor. The most outspoken critic of Russia's actions has been Singapore, which condemned the invasion and imposed sanctions on Moscow, but even Singapore abstained on the resolution suspending Russia from the UNHRC.[12] Indonesia, which chaired the Group of 20 (G20) in 2022, was subjected to Western pressure to not invite Russia to the group's summit held in Bali in November that year, but refused, offering, as a compromise solution, to invite Ukraine to the meeting. Indonesia, though condemning the invasion, pointedly refused to mention Russia by name when it did so.

In South Asia the situation is not too different. Bangladesh, India and Pakistan refused to condemn Russia's actions. India, which sees itself as a leader of the Global South, has been adamant in its reluctance to align itself on the Russia-Ukraine war.[13] This has been irksome to the US, which had undertaken a charm offensive of sorts towards India in recent years. Prime Minister Narendra Modi and President Donald Trump exchanged visits in September 2019 and February 2020, respectively. The Indian Prime Minister also visited the White House to take part in the first summit of the Quadrilateral Security Dialogue ("the Quad") in March 2021. The Quad is a military alliance formed by the US, Australia, Japan and India. With India occupying center stage in Washington's Indo-Pacific strategy, and the Quad being referred to by some (with a certain amount of hyperbole) as "Asia's NATO," the US assumption was that India would be on board with NATO's position on the war in Ukraine. But it was not. In fact, India has stepped up its oil purchases from Russia, despite the imposition of US sanctions on trade with Russia. India has thus played a key role in boosting Russia's exports and access to hard currency in difficult times, and in facilitating its remarkable economic resilience, much against the predictions that Western sanctions would make its economy crumble. From importing less than 1 percent of its oil from Russia before the war, by 2023, 40 percent of India's imported oil came from there.[14]

This leads us to the fact that the real pushback from the Global South against the Western stance on the war in Ukraine came not so much on the floor of the UNGA in votes on resolutions of various kinds, but against the diplomatic, economic and financial sanctions against Russia. Imposed unilaterally by the US and its Western allies, almost no country in Africa, Asia and Latin America, with isolated exceptions like Costa Rica and Singapore, went along with them.

Why has this been the case? What explains this remarkable gap between North and South on one of the defining issues of our time?

The West versus the Rest

Events in Ukraine have given new life and provided a badly needed unity of purpose to the Western alliance, expressed in groupings like the G7 and NATO. The renewed resolve and impetus among these Global North entities has been welcome by Western leaders. In the wake of the Summit for Democracy held in Washington on December 10, 2021, US President Joseph R. Biden, without missing a beat, proceeded to cast what would become the war in Ukraine as part and parcel of the worldwide struggle between democracy and authoritarianism, between good and evil, in language reminiscent of that of the 1950s and 1960s pitting the Free World against Soviet communism.

Put in those terms, the reaction of so much of the developing world (85 percent of the world's population lives in countries that have rejected the application of Western sanctions on Russia) becomes even more puzzling. Do these countries not realize what is at stake in Ukraine? Why can't they take a clear stance on an issue that appears to be so clear-cut, and act accordingly?

Yet, on closer examination, the issue is far from clear-cut. In fact, some of the largest and most populous democracies in the world, like India, Indonesia, Pakistan, Bangladesh, South Africa, Brazil, Mexico and Argentina, have *not* sided with Ukraine in this conflict. This makes the claim about the supposed cleavage between democracy and authoritarianism revealed by this war a questionable proposition. Not surprisingly, the argument has been made that this unwillingness to take sides reflects some sort of indecisiveness on the part of national leaders, a shameful behavior, or, worse, a moral failure at a time of reckoning.[15]

Yet, far from bringing to the fore a cleavage between democracy and authoritarianism, or some sort of character defect on the part of Global South leaders, what the war in Ukraine has exposed is something very different: the fact that the main divide in the world today is between the Global North and the Global South. Much as the G7 was given a new lease on life by Russia's actions, the stark reality is that leading countries in the South have refused to take sides in this war, reflecting the disconnect between the developed and the developing world.

There are, of course, differences in these perceptions across the South, and we'll get to them below. However, a first cut at an explanation for this apparently counterintuitive behavior of so many countries across the developing world would start by questioning the assertion that the war in Ukraine presents a unique and unprecedented challenge to the "rules-based international order." According to this reasoning, failure to condemn Russian action in the strongest terms would open the door to many more violations of this order, and the crumbling of any semblance of a peaceful international system. The war in Ukraine is a great tragedy and Russia's unprovoked aggression of a neighboring, sovereign nation should be deplored. That said, the notion that this is a "unique" war is untenable. In the past seventy years (that is, in the aftermath of World War II), many wars have taken place, mostly in Africa and Asia, several of them unprovoked and initiated by NATO member states themselves. In the recent past, a war in Yemen raged for eight years, leading to the deaths of 250,000 Yemenites – a war waged with weapons supplied by leading NATO member states. In none of these conflicts, whether in Afghanistan, Iraq or Yemen, has this led to assertions about the "unique" nature of such wars and the need for their universal condemnation, let alone for the imposition of global sanctions on the aggressor nation. On the contrary, they were considered as part and parcel of the regular order of business in the management of international relations, as is best illustrated by the case of the invasion of Iraq in 2003. The answer to the question, "Who was prosecuted for the war in Iraq?," which led to the loss of hundreds of thousands of Iraqi lives, as well as to that of 4,000 American servicemen and women, is, "no one," though it was a war waged under false pretenses (Saddam Hussein's famous "Weapons of Mass Destruction" turned out, of course, not to exist) and with no basis in international law.

What, then, is so "unique" about the war in Ukraine?

What is so unique about it is that it is taking place in Europe. And, as Indian Foreign Minister S. Jaishankar has so eloquently put it, "Europe has to grow out of the mindset that Europe's problems are the world's problems, but the world's problems are not Europe's."[16] Just because the war is taking place in the Old Continent does not mean that the whole world has to pitch in and provide Kiev with whatever it needs to counter Russian aggression. Western hypocrisy about the "rules-based order" (RBO) has rubbed many countries in the Global South the wrong way. But so has the extraordinary effort to make the Ukraine war into what Juan Gabriel Tokatlian has called the first truly global war.[17]

The deployment of unilateral political, diplomatic, economic and financial sanctions against Russia has reached unprecedented levels, making many countries realize that, if that can be done to Moscow today, it may very well be done to them tomorrow. The exclusion of Russia from the SWIFT banking system, the connecting tissue of international banking, is Exhibit A of this Western offensive, as has been the freezing of $300 billion in Russian financial assets abroad, as well as the decision to divert the proceeds of these assets to Ukraine.[18] There is, of course, nothing "rules-based" in any of these decisions. They are all unilateral actions imposed by those who control the levers of power in the established order. Thus, the push by the BRICS countries and others to de-dollarize international trade and international transactions more generally, as the use of the US dollar (USD) becomes an ever more perilous undertaking, subject to the whims of Western capitals.[19]

A distinction thus needs to be made between the condemnation of Russia's action in invading Ukraine, which most countries in the Global South have done, and the subsequent sanctions imposed by the West on Russia, which almost none of them have accepted.

Requiem for the West? The Global South and ANA

What the response from some of the leading Latin American nations (as well as from others in Africa and Asia) to the war in Ukraine shows is what we have called Active Non-Alignment (ANA).[20] By this we referred originally to a foreign policy doctrine and conceptual tool for Latin American countries to contend with the challenges posed by the US-China competition for hegemony, specifically the pressure to pick sides. The most obvious expression of this pressure was the campaign by the first Trump administration to force Latin American countries to kill projects with Chinese participation and curtail their trade, financial, technological and investment ties with China. The pressure was exercised across the board, with the visits by US government authorities to Latin America in the years of the first Trump administration being dedicated almost exclusively to pushing back on links with China. As one Central American diplomat put it, "While the Chinese talk development, all the US does is talk about China. They sound like a jealous ex-boyfriend."[21]

Several cases stand out as especially egregious examples, in particular that of the trans-Pacific, fiber optic internet cable from Chile to China. This Chilean initiative triggered by the absence of any kind of submarine internet cable across the South Pacific (meaning that all electronic communications between Asia and South America had to be routed via North America, with the consequent delayed latency and additional expense) led in January 2016 to the signing in Beijing of a Memorandum of Understanding (MOU) between the Chilean Ministry of Transport and Telecommunications and China's National Development and Reform Commission (NDRC). The understanding committed both countries to study the issue and evaluate its feasibility. Chile's status, according to some measures, as the most digitalized country in Latin America put it in an ideal situation to become China's digital gateway to

South America. A pre-feasibility study was undertaken in 2017, exploring various alternative routes across the Pacific, and concluding that installing a 20,000 km long submarine cable from Valparaíso to Shanghai would cost around $500 million – a tidy sum, but not exactly prohibitive in the context of a bilateral Chile-China trade that reached $65 billion in 2023. In 2018, there was a change of government in Chile, and the project continued on its way through the Chilean bureaucracy awaiting the next step, which was the calling of a tender for an actual feasibility study, i.e., an examination of the commercial viability of the project.[22]

Enter the first Trump administration. In April 2019, US Secretary of State Mike Pompeo led off in Chile a South American tour. In Santiago, he read the riot act to the Chilean government, threatening that all hell would break loose were Chile to go through with the fiber optic cable project connecting it to China. This led to something short of a diplomatic incident, with former Chilean President Eduardo Frei stating "Chile cannot let itself be pressured by anybody."[23] Yet, despite Frei's protestations, shortly thereafter Chile cancelled the project, later replacing it with a project for an internet cable to Australia – a country with which Chile has almost no trade – to be built and managed by Google. As of this writing, eight years after the signing of the Chile-China MOU in Beijing, there is still no internet cable connecting Asia and South America, and there are no indications that there will be one soon.[24] This is an extraordinary situation at the height of the digital age, made even more remarkable by the fact that, as we shall see in Chapter 6, China is by now South America's number-one trading partner, having displaced both the US and Europe.

Another case is that of Ecuador. One of the countries worst hit by the COVID-19 pandemic – so much so that in April 2020 bodies were piling up in the streets of Guayaquil, its largest city, because the morgues were full – it also experienced severe financial difficulties. Having at some point gone into default – and thus been excluded from capital markets, relied on China as a lender of last resort, and gone through several International Monetary Fund (IMF) structural adjustment programs and belt-tightening exercises that led to mass demonstrations and urban rioting in 2019–20 – the country was at the end of its tether. Suddenly, in January 2021, the International Financial Development Corporation (IDFC), an agency of the US government, provided it with a loan of $3.5 billion, just weeks before elections in Ecuador and in the last days of the first Trump administration. The loan was designed to tide over Ecuador's foreign debt obligations, but it came with two conditions: (1) keeping any Chinese technology out of Ecuador's telecommunications grid; and (2) privatizing $3.5 billion in assets from Ecuador's public sector, assets to be determined not solely by the Ecuadorean government, but jointly with the IDFC, opening all sorts of questions about the transparency of such a process. This was bad development policy, taking advantage of a small country going through a bad patch, and aimed at limiting its state capacity and curtailing its digital progress (as it happens Chinese 5G technology in telecommunications is both the most advanced and the most cost-effective).[25]

There are many other instances of such US pressure on Latin American countries, with Panama being another country subjected to it, and paying a significant price in terms of cancelled and/or delayed major infrastructure projects. The presence of Chinese telecommunications company Huawei in Latin America has been a matter of special concern to Washington, and has led to a variety of efforts to block its activities, though mostly to no avail.[26]

This is not to say that China has strayed far behind in exercising strong pressure on Latin American countries to toe its line. Some years ago, in protest at anti-dumping measures imposed by Argentina on certain Chinese goods, China imposed a six-month freeze on the import of Argentine soybean oil, leading to a 60 percent drop in sales to China in the first eight months of 2010. For Argentina, at the time the biggest soybean oil producer and exporter in the world, this was a major blow.[27] In an election year, this could have easily cost President Cristina Fernández de Kirchner the presidency, had it not been for India's timely one-off offer to buy most of that year's Argentine soybean harvest. In Chile, both Ambassador Xu Bu (2018–20) and his successor Niu Qingbao (2021–) have been known to play hardball as they mince no words in their dealings with the Chilean government, business and the media.[28] Ambassador Niu has been especially vocal in his criticism of one of the major projects of the government of President Gabriel Boric, a joint venture between CODELCO, Chile's state-owned copper company, and SQM, a private lithium producer, arguing that it harms the interests of Tianqi Lithium, a Chinese company that owns 25 percent of SQM.[29] The same goes for his strong protestations against the imposition of special tariffs on Chinese steel products into Chile, raising the concern of Chilean business that this might lead to some sort of Chinese retaliation against Chilean exports. Given that 40 percent of Chilean exports go to China, this puts Chile in an especially vulnerable position.

It is in this context that ANA comes to the fore. The term "active" alludes to a foreign policy in permanent search of opportunities in a changing world, analyzing each of them on their own terms. ANA acknowledges the historical roots of non-alignment but adapts them to the realities of the new century. It demands an especially deft and fine-tuned foreign policy, one closely in touch with the newly emerging challenges in the international environment.

ANA calls on Latin American governments to not accept *a priori* the stance of any of the competing Great Powers, but to act according to their own sovereign interests without giving in to political, diplomatic or economic pressures from these powers. Taking a page from the tradition of the twentieth-century Non-Aligned Movement (NAM) – whose origin was the 1955 Bandung Conference in Indonesia, led by Jawaharlal Nehru, Gamal Abdel Nasser, Sukarno and others – but reshaping it to respond to the imperatives of the new century, ANA underscores the urgency to think outside the box and come up with ways for developing nations to avoid being ever more marginalized and sidelined in a conflict-ridden and troubled world. Although originally triggered by Latin America's 2020 crisis, in which the region's GDP had its biggest downturn in 120 years,[30] from the beginning the concept has referred to a broader spatial and temporal scope: it applies across the Global South as a whole and is pertinent for situations of hegemonic conflict in general.

Thus, though inspired by the Autonomy School of Latin American International Relations, embodied in authors such as Hélio Jaguaribe and Juan Carlos Puig, ANA also recognizes what the World Bank has called the shift in wealth from the North Atlantic to the Asia-Pacific that has taken place since the early 2000s.[31] According to various projections, in 2050, the three largest economies in the world will be China, India and the US, in that order. Also, by that year, among the world's top ten economies, seven will be non-Western. Rather than speaking from weakness, as the Third World did in the 1970s and 1980s when it deployed its *diplomatie des cahiers des doléances* (victimhood diplomacy) in pushing for the New International Economic Order (NIEO), the New South now uses "collective financial statecraft," relying on entities such as the Asian Investment and Infrastructure Bank (AIIB) and the New Development Bank (NDB, the so-called "BRICS Bank"), which offer new opportunities for emerging and developing economies.

There is thus a radically new environment in which developing nations find themselves able to increase their options and alternatives vis-à-vis the Great Powers. The US-China tensions that have put Latin America between a rock and a hard place, and the war in Ukraine that has brought to the fore the extant differences between the West and some of the leading countries in Africa, Asia and Latin America, are thus part and parcel of a broader pattern of the changing world order, one of whose distinct features is that of the rise of the Global South. It is for many of these countries that ANA emerges as an almost natural foreign policy option.

In this context, the questions arise: How real is this option? Aren't weaker states, almost by definition, at the mercy of the Great Powers?

To answer these questions we need to dwell a bit further on the margin of maneuver weaker and smaller states now enjoy in foreign policy.

Great Powers and weaker states

"The strong do what they can and the weak suffer what they must." Thucydides' well-worn dictum has been something of an axiom in the study of International Relations, ever since he first formulated it in his study of the Peloponnesian War.[32]

This has been reinforced by the fact that much of the literature in the discipline has emerged in the US and in Europe, with a focus on the role and actions of the Great Powers, seemingly confirming the notion that there is little room for maneuver for weaker states in the international system. In the more recent past, Henry Kissinger was convinced that History (with a capital H) took place solely in the Northern Hemisphere, and nothing of significance happened in the South.[33] In this perspective, there is little the vast majority of states in the world (most of which are located in Africa, Asia and Latin America) can do to escape from the subjugation to the Great Powers. And it is this perception that partly explains the generalized surprise of Western observers and commentators at the reaction of so many of these states to the (failed) attempt by the West to make the war in Ukraine a global war against Russia.

Yet, this notion fails to capture the very different roles and interests of Great Powers and weaker states in the international system. Whereas the Great Powers have the capacity and the ability to affect the very nature and direction of the international system, act accordingly, and consider their main threats to come from the actions of other Great Powers, weaker states are in a very different position. They have little or no capacity to affect the international system. They tend to be still in a developing condition and have serious difficulties in fully exercising a monopoly of force within their borders. For them, the main threat does not necessarily come from other powers, but from the international environment more broadly, in the form of financial crises, pandemics, natural disasters and other such phenomena. As Kassab has pointed out, the condition of weaker states is marked by their *vulnerability* and lack of *resilience*, that is, their exposure to outside shocks and inability to absorb them and recover quickly.[34] Their main concern is thus not with military power or international standing, as is the case with the Great Powers, but with economic development and improving the welfare of their citizens, many of whom live in dire straits.

However, it is this very weakness that, paradoxically, creates an opening for weaker states to make the most of an otherwise hostile and uncertain international system. As the individual action of any one of them is too insignificant to affect the balance of power between the Great Powers, they enjoy sufficient policy space not to feel (at least not absolutely) restricted to the established spheres of influence, and can thus, as it were, play both sides against the middle. It was precisely the emergence of many weak post-colonial states in the 1950s and 1960s that gave rise to the Non-Aligned Movement. And it is the transition from the unipolar moment to this new era of Great Power competition that makes it imperative for these weaker states to come up with a compass to navigate these perilous waters. Hence the comeback of non-alignment, albeit this time in a new incarnation, as Active Non-Alignment, the subject of this book. As pointed out above, though, a crucial difference between the original non-alignment and today's ANA lies in the much stronger position in which the South finds itself, of which the BRICS+ is Exhibit A.[35]

This convergence by countries in the Global South, though still quite short of what we might call concerted collective action, has triggered some pushback from Western commentators and think tanks. Revealingly, this pushback has been not so much against the policy positions espoused by these various groups, as against the use of the term "Global South";[36] in other words, denying the very existence of any such thing, although the term has been in use for over half a century now, university courses are taught on the subject and there is an extensive literature on it.[37] Much of the criticism of the term is directed at its alleged geographical imprecision (since countries like China and India are in the Northern not the Southern Hemisphere), though this ignores the fact that the term has never been a strictly geographical one. Rather, it has always been a geopolitical and geohistorical one, referring to countries, mostly in Africa, Asia and Latin America, that tend to be poorer, that have a colonial past and that are often economically dependent on developed countries. Another criticism of the term is that it is polarizing, and should thus be discontinued, as it does not contribute to international peace and harmony. This is a bit rich coming from quarters that regularly praise the renewed unity and resolve of the G7 and of NATO as a significant achievement, and somehow do not consider this Western belligerence, exposed so dramatically in the Israel/Gaza war, as polarizing at all.

Some of the Global South countries have done well economically, but this is not yet reflected in the power structures of existing international organizations like the UN or the Bretton Woods institutions. This does not mean that they all see eye-to-eye on this issue. Rising powers like India, Brazil and Turkey bring different perspectives to the table, and have enjoyed more access to the rarefied higher echelons of global governance than, say, Mali or Paraguay. But the notion that they are still mere interlopers persists. This is a longstanding source of grievance in the Global South, which leads us to yet another expression of the North-South cleavage alluded to earlier. Moreover, there seems to be no learning curve. At the 2024 G7 Summit, held in Italy, the host country invited several leaders from rising powers to attend as guests, presumably to share their grievances and plead with the G7 member leaders to act on them. Yet, this is precisely the model of global governance and North-South cooperation that fell apart in 2004–5, when G7 Summit hosts did the same with the leaders of China, India and Brazil, among other countries, inviting them for the breakfast session, and then sending them off so that the "serious countries" could go on with the real business of managing economic global governance. As such haughty behavior became unsustainable, the creation of the G20 at leaders' level in 2008 was one response. Yet, twenty years on, the world seems to have gone back to square one.

This is happening at a time when the differences between North and South are sharpening, and many countries are striking out on their own, not letting themselves be cajoled into siding automatically with one or another of the Great Powers simply because that is what they are expected to do.

Conclusion

A longstanding source of grievance in developing nations is Western hypocrisy – the double standard applied by Western nations to their own behavior and to that of other countries. Seldom has this hypocrisy been more apparent than in the Israel/Gaza war. As one senior G7 diplomat put it: "We have definitely lost the battle for the Global South. All the work we have done with the Global South (over Ukraine) has been lost . . . Forget about rules, forget about world order. They won't ever listen to us again."[38]

That said, it is important to understand that the wars in Ukraine and in Gaza are not the *cause* for this "Southern discontent" with the existing world order, but rather *symptoms* of a far deeper malaise arising from the extant international arrangements. The much-vaunted "rules-based international order" the West says it is so keen to uphold has done little to contend with some of the world's key global challenges – climate change, financial indebtedness, mass migrations, pandemics and others – while the West seemingly remains focused solely on its own priorities: mostly competing with China, and now with Russia. The Ukraine and Gaza wars have only brought to the fore this harsh reality. It is in such a context that ANA emerges as the most suitable response from the South to a deeply troubled world.

Yet, what is ANA exactly? How does it translate into a specific approach to foreign policy and to handling the abovementioned challenges? That is the subject of the next chapter, to which we now turn.

2

What is Active Non-Alignment and What Fuels It?

On December 29, 2023, South Africa initiated proceedings against Israel at the International Court of Justice (ICJ) in The Hague, with a case entitled "Application of the Convention on the Prevention and Punishment of the Crime of Genocide in the Gaza Strip (South Africa vs Israel)."[1] In it, South Africa alleges that Israel is engaging in genocide against the Palestinians in Gaza through "acts and omissions" that are "intended to bring about the destruction of a substantial part of the Palestinian national, racial and ethnic group." Israel has denied the claims and argued that it has taken a variety of measures to protect the lives of Palestinian civilians, such as warning them in advance of air strikes and aborting some strikes when civilians are present in targeted areas. On January 26, 2024, in what are known as "emergency measures," the ICJ ruled that it is plausible that Israel is committing genocide in Gaza, and instructed the State of Israel to take all measures within its powers to prevent the commission of genocide, but it did not order Israel to halt all operations in Gaza, as South Africa had requested.[2]

Cases at the ICJ typically take years to be resolved, and it is unlikely that these legal proceedings – which the Court has no way to enforce in any case – will have any immediate effect on Israeli ground operations in Gaza, which have continued unabated in the aftermath of the Court's ruling. That said, there is little doubt that the very fact of South Africa bringing such a case to the ICJ – accusing Israel, a state whose origin was at least partly based on the need to remedy the tragedy of the Holocaust in World War II, that is, the annihilation of 6 million Jews in the gas chambers of the Third Reich – had considerable symbolic significance. The case has tarnished the standing and the reputation of a country routinely described as "the only democracy in the Middle East" and widely considered to be a key Western ally in that part of the world.

The fact that the case was brought by South Africa, a vibrant African democracy whose transition from apartheid rule in the 1990s is considered one of the emblematic transitions from authoritarian rule of that decade, gave this initiative additional significance and normative power. Nelson Mandela, the first President of South Africa's new dispensation, and a great champion of the Palestinian cause (as he put it in 1997: "We know only too well that our freedom is incomplete without the freedom of Palestinians"),[3] is of course an icon of the struggle for racial justice in the twentieth century. Ten countries from the Global South presented *amicus curiae* submissions to the ICJ, adhering to the South African position, making a total of fifty nations from Africa, Asia and Latin America expressing their support for the case. In turn, Western powers, such as the US and Germany (which presented an *amicus curiae* brief to the Court in *support* of Israel), stood firmly by Israel.[4]

While this was happening in The Hague, across the Atlantic, at United Nations headquarters in New York, a similar dynamic was taking place. At the United Nations General Assembly, on October 27, 2023, 121 states supported an immediate humanitarian ceasefire in Gaza, with fourteen voting against it and forty-four abstaining; on December 12, 153 voted in favor of an unconditional ceasefire, ten voted against and twenty-three abstained.[5] As chair of the United Nations Security Council

(UNSC), in late October Brazil presented a resolution calling for a ceasefire in Gaza, a resolution that was vetoed by the US. Two additional such resolutions were subsequently submitted to the UNSC, also vetoed by the US.

Gaza, Israel and the Global South

Just as the Russian invasion of Ukraine failed to trigger the unanimous condemnation across the developing world that Western leaders expected, the Israel-Hamas war in Gaza, and the unlimited support provided by the US and the EU to Israel (highlighted by immediate visits to Jerusalem by President Biden and EU Commission head Ursula von der Layen), went down badly in Africa, Asia and Latin America. At the October 26, 2023, United Nations General Assembly vote calling for a "humanitarian truce" in the war in Gaza, 120 countries voted in favor, while a mere fourteen voted against, including the US and four members of the EU. Forty-five members abstained, including fifteen members of the EU, plus the United Kingdom, Canada, Australia and Japan. The North-South split could not have been starker.

The horrific attack on Israeli military and civilians by Hamas on October 7, 2023, which led to 1,200 deaths and the taking of 240 hostages, was widely condemned, but what was incomprehensible across the Global South was the active Western support for Israel's ensuing attacks on Gaza, which caused 11,000 deaths, 4,000 of them children, in the following five weeks. Key rising powers from the Global South were among the most vocal critics of Israel on this occasion. They included Turkey and Indonesia, both with large Muslim populations, but countries like Brazil and South Africa also joined the fray.

Historically, many African and Asian countries have supported the Palestinian cause. Indonesia does not even recognize Israel. But Latin America's reaction to Israel's actions in

Gaza has been also very critical. In short order, Bolivia broke off relations with Israel, and Chile and Colombia called their ambassadors from Jerusalem for consultations – a traditional diplomatic tool to show disapproval of a country's behavior. Shortly thereafter, Belize suspended its diplomatic relations with Israel, recalling its ambassador and retracting its request for accreditation for an honorary consul in Tel Aviv. Brazil, as chair of the UNSC, introduced the resolution supporting a ceasefire in Gaza. In May 2024, it withdrew its ambassador from Israel.

Brazil has labeled the campaign in Gaza a "genocide" – a comment echoed by South Africa's government when it recalled its ambassador from Israel in protest. While the US has used the term "genocide" to refer to Russia's action in Ukraine, the Biden administration has specifically said it does not apply to Israel's action in Gaza.

By August 2024, it was estimated that some 40,000 people had been killed in Gaza by Israeli attacks, of which some 16,000 were children.[6] More children were killed in Gaza in four months after October 7, 2023, than in all wars in the world in the past four years.[7] Yet, the West – with some honorable exceptions, like Ireland, Slovenia, Norway and Spain (the latter joining South Africa with an *amicus curia* at its case against Israel at the ICJ) – and especially the US, continued its unwavering support for Israel, not just rhetorically and at the UN, but also militarily by providing it with the bombs and weapons that make the carnage in Gaza possible.

Revealingly, references to the rules-based order, so common in the case of the war in Ukraine, have vanished from Western discourse on Gaza, being replaced by arguments on "the need for Israel to defend itself."

The contrast between the concern expressed in Western capitals for the humanitarian suffering inflicted on Ukrainians by the war with Russia, and the acquiescence to and downright complicity with the suffering inflicted upon Palestinians by

Israel's war on Gaza, could not be greater. In many ways, much as the war in Ukraine brought to the fore the extant cleavage between the Global North and the Global South, the war in Gaza has underlined the vacuity of the Western discourse on the defense of human rights as a universal concept. As one analyst put it, "the charge is the west writes the rules to suit itself. If countries which support Ukraine and are working for peace in the Middle East do not realize how powerful this charge has become, they will fail to solve either conflict."[8]

In this regard, it is significant that in the case of the war in Gaza it is countries from the Global South that have taken the lead in opposition to it, with Brazil submitting the resolution for a ceasefire in October 2023, and South Africa taking its case against Israel to the ICJ in December that year. Both initiatives were resisted by the West, despite the extraordinary humanitarian suffering on the ground in Gaza.

Thus, in Gaza, the Western grand narrative about the proclaimed universality of human rights and the significance of defending them wherever they are violated has been shown to be hollow. As Gaza indicates, for the West the defense of human rights only holds when it comes to protecting the rights of those considered Westerners, or when such rights can be weaponized against adversaries. Otherwise, they are irrelevant. Why the difference in the dissimilar concerns about the fate of Ukrainians and Palestinians? The reason is very simple. Ukrainians are Europeans, Palestinians are not. Moreover, as Colombian President Gustavo Petro put it, "Germany . . . France, the European Union, the United Kingdom and above all the United States of America . . . support dropping bombs on people because they are making a demonstration in front of the whole of humanity, that what happens to Palestine can happen to any of you if you dare to make changes without their permission."[9]

Part of the legitimacy of this international order had been based on a grand, post-World War II narrative about promoting democracy and human rights as "forces of good," versus dictatorship and authoritarianism as "forces of evil."[10] The reality, of course, was more complex than this, with the West propping up dictators across the world, as long as they stood against communism. Yet, by and large, the illusion of this grand narrative persisted, and appeared to find further confirmation with the fall of the Berlin Wall.[11]

However, in the new century, that narrative is crumbling before our eyes, exposed by what is seen in the Global South as Western hypocrisy and myopia, made so evident in Gaza. As Malaysia's Prime Minister, Anwar Ibrahim, put it in a recent visit to Germany: "We oppose colonialism, or apartheid or ethnic cleansing or dispossession of any country, be it in Ukraine or in Gaza. Where have we thrown our humanity? Why this hypocrisy?"[12] Germany's steadfast support of Israel, at the ICJ and as a weapons supplier, has also brought to the fore another genocide committed by Germans – that of the Herero and Nama people in Namibia in 1904–8, considered the twentieth century's first genocide, with some 70,000 fatal victims. As Namibian President Hage Geingob put it, Germany cannot "morally express commitment to the United Nations Convention Against Genocide, including atonement for the genocide in Namibia, and at the same time support Israel."[13]

A post-colonial grand narrative

Namibia's claim in this regard is of special significance, as it underscores a major shift in the grand narratives of global politics.[14] As mentioned above, in the aftermath of World War II, and in parallel to the establishment of the liberal international order (LIO), a certain "short-term" narrative on world affairs was installed and became dominant. In it, the central dynamic in international relations was the one between the forces of democracy and freedom – i.e., Western democracies, with the US and the UK at their core – and those of totalitarianism and oppression, epitomized by the Soviet Union and the socialist camp. Much of the evil in the world was attributed to the latter, and those who sided with it.[15] After the fall of the Soviet Union, and the failure of half-hearted attempts to bring its successor state, i.e. Russia, into the European fold, this grand narrative has now been revived, with countries like China, Russia and Iran embodying the equivalent of a new "axis of evil."

Initiatives like the "Summit for Democracy" spearheaded by the US, which has been meeting since 2021 in various capitals, reflect this attempt to present the world with what appears to be a binary choice between democracy and autocracy, between freedom and oppression.[16] The problem is that this apparent support for democracy around the world is no more than a façade. Of the fifty nations that Freedom House defined as dictatorships in 2023, thirty-five receive military aid from the US.[17] Under these circumstances, it is not difficult to see why this discourse finds few takers in the Global South, where it is viewed as little more than a thinly disguised veil to foster Western strategic objectives. In this context, the US-Saudi link, one that cuts across Republican and Democratic administrations, is Exhibit A.

Not surprisingly, what the war in Ukraine, and even more so the one in Gaza, have brought to the fore is a different, more "long-term" post-colonial narrative on the dynamic of international relations in our time.[18] In this perspective, the roots of the current state of world affairs reach much deeper than 1945, and go back all the way to the age of empire and colonialism. There is a reason why Israeli settler efforts to displace Palestinians from their land in the West Bank, let alone statements about having their eyes set on the Gaza Strip and its beaches, trigger so much pushback in South Africa. That is exactly what settler colonialism did in South Africa with the native population there.

In this perspective, illustrated by China's references to its own "century of humiliation" (1839–1949), Western powers, far from embodying beacons of freedom and human progress occupying the moral high ground in the forward march of history, represent something very different. They are none other than the successors of empires that brought much suffering and oppression to the peoples of Africa, Asia and Latin America, legacies with which these nations are forced to cope to this day.

The new non-alignment

It is in this context that what has been called "the new non-alignment," and we call Active Non-Alignment (ANA), has risen to the fore. The end of the unipolar moment, and the shift towards what Amitav Acharya has referred to as a multiplex world,[19] has been marked by a confluence of factors leading to a polycrisis.[20] Pandemics, wars, climate change, financial instability, mass migrations, water scarcity and food insecurity are only some of them. The inability (and/or unwillingness) of the Great Powers to manage these global challenges has led to a general discontent across much of the developing world as well as to a search for new responses to the pressures these countries are being subjected to.

As discussed in Chapter 1, ANA arose in Latin America as a response to the region's deep health and economic crisis of 2020. This crisis overlapped with the rise of tensions between Washington and Beijing, tensions that reached the lands South of the Rio Grande, as both powers tried to impose their will on them. A widespread, though by no means unanimous, reaction to this in Latin America was for governments to hedge their bets. There was a refusal to take sides, and a very self-conscious decision to take each issue on its merits, and to choose accordingly. Albeit not necessarily articulated as such in foreign policy speeches, in Latin America 2022 was very much, as *Foreign Policy* put it, the year of Active Non-Alignment.[21]

How so?

ANA corresponds to a certain foreign policy strategy, one that deals with what Arnold Wolfers referred to as "milieu goals." By these he meant goals related to the management of the external environment of any given state, as distinct from what he called "possession goals," which refer to the defense of the state's own core interests in the security, military or economic spheres.[22] While the two are interrelated, milieu goals refer to a more proactive stance in attempting to shape this environment and give it a certain direction, going beyond the strictly defensive maneuvers required by a Hobbesian world.

In the period immediately following World War II, and with the onset of decolonization, many countries achieved their national independence. In doing so, they found themselves embroiled in the Cold War and the heightened tensions between the two emerging superpowers – the US and the Soviet Union – tensions overshadowed by the ominous specter of nuclear conflagration. In addition to the challenges associated with a newly acquired national sovereignty, many countries in Africa, Asia and the Caribbean had to deal with the pressures coming from this bipolar system. One response to this was the rise of the Non-Aligned Movement, formally launched in Belgrade in 1961.[23] The NAM sought to provide a space for these post-colonial states, embracing a variety of principles like respect for national sovereignty, non-intervention, non-adherence to military alliances with any of the superpowers, peaceful coexistence and adherence to multilateralism and the UN.[24]

Our argument is that, as the international system shifts towards a "multiplex system," albeit one marked by a certain bipolar imprint in which the US and China play a key role and compete on a variety of fronts, a different expression of the non-alignment of yesteryear has come to the fore, this time in the form of what we call ANA. The key point about ANA is that it is not a movement, but a certain type of foreign policy behavior that attempts to deal with an uncertain environment. As indicated in the previous chapter, it arose initially in Latin America in 2019–20, in the context of the COVID-19 pandemic and its devastating effects, and the biggest economic downturn the region had experimented in 120 years. It then also came to the fore in Africa and Asia, that is, across the rest of the Global South, in the aftermath of the wars in Ukraine and in Gaza, expressing itself, among other ways, in the expansion of the BRICS group. As Indian analyst Shivshankar Menon puts it: "when the international system is failing or absent, and when it seems to be each country for itself, it is no surprise that leaders turn to non-alignment."[25]

ANA and "playing the field"

Yet, what does non-alignment mean in practice in the twenty-first century? As discussed in the previous chapter, ANA does not equal neutrality, a legal concept that refers to the position states take in relation to the parties in a war situation. Neither does it represent mere equidistance between the Great Powers in competition. On the contrary, ANA embodies a dynamic foreign policy approach that may lead states to side with one or another of the Great Powers, depending on the issue.

In the international relations (IR) literature, the traditional approaches to dealing with other powers have been described as "balancing" and "bandwagoning." By *balancing* is meant taking a hard position against a certain power; *bandwagoning*, on the other hand, means aligning yourself completely with a certain power. Weaker powers, of course, are hardly able to take hard stances against Great Powers, so balancing is largely out of bounds. The underlying assumption has thus been that weaker powers don't have much choice but to bandwagon.

Yet, this does not do justice to actual state behavior. In situations of Great Power competition, like the current one, these powers build their own spheres of influence and aim to win over the hearts and minds of other international actors to enhance their own standing and reputation. This dynamic, in turn, opens possibilities for weaker states to benefit and make the most of the windows of opportunity such competition entails. This is reinforced by the very different concerns and motivations of the Great Powers and of weaker states. As discussed above, the main threat to Great Powers comes from the action of other Great Powers. Their security and military prowess are, thus, their priority. For weaker states, on the other hand, the main threats emanate from their general vulnerability to external shocks of various kinds, which are enhanced in a globalized and interdependent world. These shocks can originate in financial crises, pandemics, natural disasters or in broader phenomena like climate change – that may lead to the very disappearance from the face of the Earth of some of them, like the Pacific Island states.

In these circumstances, the main concern of weaker states is development and economic progress, so that they can overcome this vulnerability and lack of resilience to external shocks.[26] Given their lack of resources, they appeal to the Great Powers, seeking to bolster their trade, investment and financial cooperation links with them. In their efforts to "bind" weaker states, Great Powers may acquiesce to such appeals, on the understanding that refusals may lead the petitioner to knock on the door of the competition. In a situation with a declining hegemon and a rising power threatening that hegemony, like the one taking place between the US and China, this dynamic is accentuated, with the rising power being especially motivated to "bribe" weaker states to enhance its own standing in the international system. In turn, the very decline of hegemony feeds on itself, often leading the hegemon to retreat from exercising the duties normally associated with hegemony, such as the provision of global public goods, and to hide behind a fortress of protectionism and isolationism.

ANA thus makes it possible for weaker states to leverage this situation for their own benefit, through what Hanna Samir Kassab has called "playing the field."[27] By this he means a grand strategy that purposefully plays both sides against the middle. Rather than siding with one or another of the Great Powers, the goal instead is to extract the maximum welfare and development benefits possible from both sides in the game. Our point is that the current international conjuncture is especially conducive to such an approach, in a way that was not the case in the recent past. During the Cold War, the relatively small size of the Soviet economy and its minimal foreign trade and foreign investment flows made it very difficult for the Soviet Union to compete with what the US had to offer in economic terms – though this was not the case in defense matters. And for much of the post-Cold War period, the overwhelming predominance of the US in most spheres left weaker states with little room for maneuver. Washington was the only game in town.

Yet, the rise of China in the new century has put paid to that. Since 2014, the Chinese economy has overtaken that of the US in terms of purchasing power parity (PPP), and according to some projections the Chinese GDP in market prices will be higher than that of the US by 2030. In 2024, the Chinese GDP represented 19.2 percent of global GDP. Moreover, the much more significant role of the state and the public sector in China means that Beijing can allocate resources to its foreign policy commitments in a way that the United States cannot – thus the 1 trillion-plus dollars China spent on its Belt and Road Initiative (BRI) across the world from 2013 to 2023. This means that despite the larger size of the US economy and the scientific and technological advantages the US still enjoys over China, it has been losing ground in the Global South as Beijing makes significant inroads in Africa, Asia and Latin America.

From grand strategy to tactics

ANA puts the national interest of developing nations front and center. It stands for not letting oneself be pressured into becoming "the plaything of others," in Nehru's famous phrase. On the contrary, weak states "play the field" with the Great Powers, trying to maximize the welfare benefits they can obtain. How does this work in practice?

If ANA is a foreign policy doctrine whose grand strategy is "playing the field," what are the specific tactics that follow from that? What is it that governments in general and foreign ministries in particular must *do* to implement it successfully? Can ANA be accused, as its predecessor the NAM often was, of being more about grandstanding and making highfaluting statements at international conferences than about specific foreign policy advice?

It is here that the notion of hedging comes into play. As Malaysian political scientist Cheng-Chwee Kuik indicates,[28] hedging entails taking a middle position of sorts between balancing and bandwagoning, while keeping one's options open. Sound hedging will attempt to maintain good relations with both Great Powers in conflict, nurture as many links with other powers as possible (as a form of self-insurance) and be sure to always have a fallback position. Hedging is a tool to deal with situations of high uncertainty in which outcomes are not assured and the downside of making the wrong bet can be devastating. As Brazilian scholar Matias Spektor puts it, "these countries are pursuing a strategy of hedging because they see the future distribution of global power as uncertain and wish to avoid commitments that will be hard to discharge."[29]

As a report from the European Council on Foreign Relations (ECFR), based on public opinion polling in major countries across the Global South, put it:

> They seem to prefer an *à la carte* arrangement in which their governments do not have to align and where they can pragmatically pursue their own national interests with different partners on different issues. The US and the EU on one side and China on the other are thus not perceived as competitive political models that a country needs to emulate, but as other great powers with which you can either cooperate or compete – depending on the issue.[30]

In this regard, the difference between the initial Cold War and what some today refer to as the Second Cold War is significant.[31] In the former case, international relations were very much about bloc politics, the boundaries were relatively clear, and although there were gray zones and border areas where conflicts would emerge, the lines separating the spheres of influence of each of the two superpowers were well-defined. In today's much more globalized and interdependent world, things are different. The very notion of spheres of influence has come into question, and the world resembles much more an open arena in which all can participate in the game than it does a field full of enclosures in which countries are assigned to one or another sphere, without much of a say as to which one that would be.

Latin America: playing both sides against the middle?

The case of Latin America is illustrative of this condition, as a region once regarded very much as part of the sphere of influence of the US, and now in a very different situation with the sudden irruption of China into the Western Hemisphere.

With Sino-LAC (Latin America and the Caribbean) trade having jumped from $12 billion in 2000 to $485 billion in 2023, China is by now South America's largest trading partner, as it is for individual countries like Brazil, Chile, Peru and Uruguay.[32] This creates its own set of imperatives for the management of Great Power competition in the Americas. The point is not, as it is sometimes portrayed, one of having to choose between being pro-US or pro-China. With two centuries of diplomatic relations and longstanding economic, military, cultural and even family links between the country of Uncle Sam and the lands South of the Rio Grande, most Latin Americans, and especially its elites, feel much closer to the US than they do to China, notwithstanding the dubious legacies of the Monroe Doctrine, gunboat diplomacy and more recent US interventions in the region.

The question is a different one. It alludes to the fact that, given China's dizzying rate of growth for much of this century, the notorious impact the so-called "China boom" had on the region in the decade of the commodities super-cycle (2003–13), and the complementarity between the Chinese economy and South America's, the notion that somehow Latin America could "decouple" from China, as some sectors in Washington apparently wish could happen, is untenable.[33] On the contrary, for Latin America's leaders and decision-makers, the real question is how to continue to leverage these ties with China, and thus expand trade and investment links even further. This is not to say that they have become "China-lovers" or sympathizers with the Chinese Communist Party (CCP). It simply reflects the reality that China's economic presence in the Americas in the current century has made a considerable difference on the ground through trade, investment and financial cooperation. At the same time, in many countries in the region, and especially those around the Caribbean Basin, the US remains the number-one investor in terms of foreign direct investment (FDI) stock and trade flows. In matters of defense and security, US hegemony is unabated. Thus, hedging.

Examples abound. The case of Brazil is instructive. In April 2023, President Luiz Inácio Lula da Silva visited China with a huge business delegation and an agenda to expand further the already significant Brazil-China trade, which reached $158 billion in 2023, as well as Chinese investment in Brazil, which at $75 billion represents about half of all Chinese foreign direct investment in the region. As we have seen, both on Ukraine and Gaza Brazil has taken a very different stance from that of the US, having even undertaken a peace initiative on the war in Ukraine that was not well-received in Washington.[34] At the same time, when the International Development Finance Corporation – a US-government entity set up in 2018 to counteract China's financial lending for infrastructure across the developing world in general and in Latin America in particular – set up a branch abroad, Brazil was happy to open its doors for the IDFC in São Paulo, South America's financial capital. Brazil is also "a major non-NATO ally."

Hedging is practiced both by progressive governments and by conservative ones. The heavily indebted government of Ecuador has been in dire straits and is keen to expand its access to world markets. In 2022, it approached the US government about the possibility of negotiating a bilateral free trade agreement (FTA) like the one the US already has with Ecuador's neighbors, Colombia, Peru and Chile. The Biden administration rebuffed the request, informing the government of President Guillermo Lasso that the US was not in the business of negotiating FTAs anymore. Without missing a beat, President Lasso – who in February 2022 had been one of two Latin American heads of state attending the inauguration of the Olympic Games in China, in overt defiance of the Western diplomatic boycott of the event – promptly approached Beijing with a similar request. It was well received, negotiations were quickly initiated and successfully concluded, and the China-Ecuador FTA came into effect in May 2024.[35]

In some ways the Latin American country that has most perfected the art of hedging is Chile, one of only six countries in the world to have FTAs both with the US and with China. On October 14–16, 2023, President Gabriel Boric undertook a state visit to China where he was received by President Xi, with all the pomp such visits merit in China, and participated in the Third BRI International Cooperation Forum held in Beijing. This made Chile the only Latin American country to have participated at the presidential level in all three BRI Forums held so far in Beijing, attended by three different presidents of Chile, each from a different coalition. Scarcely two weeks later, on November 2, President Boric was received at the White House by President Biden for the launch of the Americas Partnership for Economic Prosperity (APEP). Both in Beijing and in Washington, the issue of the local processing of Chile's lithium, a resource in which both US and Chinese companies have significant investments, was a key item on the agenda.[36]

Should this kind of hedging be considered opportunistic? Shouldn't foreign policy behavior be guided by principles rather than by mere interests? To what extent does ANA reflect simple opportunism, rather than a sounder approach based on a country's longstanding traditions and view of the world? The US and the EU are, of course, especially insistent on this, stressing that countries in Latin America in particular, but also elsewhere, should align their foreign policies with Western powers, with whom they share democratic values, thus providing a much stronger basis for their relations. In this context, the Biden administration came up with a more fine-tuned policy than that of the first Trump presidency, realizing that undue pressure on foreign capitals can often backfire. "Countries don't want to choose and we don't want them to," says Jake Sullivan, White House National Security Advisor.[37] Alignment with Washington should not be the result of pressures and sanctions, but a decision made of the countries' own free will, siding with like-minded partners with similar political systems. Which brings us to the issue of values.

ANA and the vexed issue of values

The secret to the success of any kind of foreign policy lies in finding the right balance between values and interests. Countries represent a certain idea of themselves that they must respect, nurture and preserve. These values are what, in the end, provide states with the leadership abilities and soft power that will allow them to build coalitions and to undertake significant international projects of various kinds. That said, countries also have material interests related to the survival of the nation, their defense needs and the protection of their natural resources and economic activities. No government can ignore these in the name of certain abstract values, no matter how significant they may be.

This leads us to a debate regarding the Third EU-CELAC (Community of Latin American and Caribbean States) Summit held in Brussels on July 17–18, 2023. A recurring theme in the weeks prior to the summit, as well as during it, was that of the presence in Latin America of the so-called "extra-regional powers," i.e., China, Russia and Iran, a list to which some would add India. The argument set forth by the European leaders, as well as by a number of Latin American analysts and commentators, was that in the recent past Latin America had gotten "dangerously" close to these powers, particularly to China, but also to Russia (a warning especially clearly expressed in the reactions to Russia's invasion of Ukraine).[38] According to this European perspective, this is something that should be reconsidered by Latin American governments, as it exposes them to all sorts of dangers coming from these authoritarian regimes.[39] Following this reasoning, the way forward for the region would be to privilege its relations with Europe, a continent with which Latin America, an overwhelmingly democratic part of the world, shares its democratic values.[40]

In principle, this seems reasonable. It should be obvious that, in terms of history, political culture and all sorts of traditions, a country like Argentina has much more in common with Germany or France (let alone Spain) than it does with either China or Russia. Yet, once we start to unpack this argument, we realize that the link between values and interests is somewhat more complex than it appears at first sight. The Third EU-CELAC Summit took place eight long years after the second one, held in 2015. As we saw in Chapter 1, these eight years were among the most difficult the region had experienced in a century, including as they did the biggest economic downturn in 120 years, and a significant health crisis in which the region, with 8 percent of the world's population, accounted for nearly 30 percent of the world's deaths.

However, in this period (during which three summits of the Americas and three China-CELAC ministerial fora took place), Europe, for all intents and purposes, simply forgot Latin America even existed. In other words, when the region was undergoing one of its most difficult moments, Europe was exclusively focused on its own problems and paid no attention whatsoever to the region's deep crisis.

What happened to these supposedly shared values at that moment?

In turn, in 2023, with a war taking place in Europe, the EU suddenly "rediscovered" Latin America and called the Third EU-CELAC Summit. The main purpose of the latter, however, was not to fix the highly deteriorated inter-regional links, let alone to work with Latin America on how to help the region come out of its difficult post-pandemic situation. Rather, its main driver was to gain support for Ukraine in its war with Russia. So much so that the keynote speaker initially invited by the EU to address the summit was none other than Volodymyr Zelensky – the

President of Ukraine – who had to be promptly disinvited, given Latin America's refusal to have him in the program.[41]

In early 2021, when in Europe different pharmaceutical companies had successfully developed anti-COVID vaccines, and Latin American countries continued to suffer the deadly effects of the virus, despite repeated entreaties from various governments in the region, Europe refused to sell them vaccines in any significant quantities, under the pretext of an overt "vaccine nationalism."[42] As if this was not enough, when, shortly thereafter, President Biden suggested that both US and European pharmaceutical companies should give up their intellectual property (IP) rights to these vaccines, so that they could also be produced in countries of the Global South and thus alleviate the health crisis, the EU opposed any such move. The reason given was that this would affect the legitimate profits to which these companies were entitled.[43]

While this extraordinary European indifference to Latin America's human tragedy played out, the so-called "extra-regional powers," i.e. China, Russia and India, engaging in what has been called "vaccine diplomacy," made significant efforts to provide vaccines to the region. The vaccines were of inferior quality to the European ones, but they did the needful and could not have arrived at a better moment. Thanks to the Sinovac vaccine provided by China, Chile managed to position itself among the four or five countries in the world with the highest share of vaccinated population. In turn, Argentina and Brazil benefited from high quantities of Indian and Russian vaccines, as well as Chinese ones.

Amazingly, in the first four months of 2021, the United States not only refused to provide vaccines to developing nations, but actively waged a disinformation campaign *against* Chinese vaccines that were being provided to countries like the Philippines.[44]

Our point is twofold. On the one hand, it is of little use to talk about "shared values" in abstract terms, if, when it comes to the crunch, those values do not translate into concrete actions responding to the national urgencies of the moment. A partnership based supposedly on shared values whose partners do not come through when they are needed has not much going for it. On the other hand, this also points to the significance of diversifying international linkages, and the added options this offers, something closely related to what ANA is all about.

Chile could not have secured the number of Chinese vaccines it did at that very critical moment had it not been for its longstanding, half-century relationship with China. This includes not just government links, but also those of business and universities, all of which played a key role in the complex operation that made it possible to save tens of thousands of lives, at a time when traditional partners like the US and Europe were not ready to step in and do the needful.

Thus, the notion that, in the new century, the way forward for Latin American countries would be to *restrict* and *limit* their international relations for the sake of an alleged commitment to democratic values does not pass muster. On the contrary, the evidence indicates that, much as the extensive literature in the IR field shows, it is by *diversifying* and *multiplying* those links – not by *restricting* them – be it in diplomacy, trade, investment or finance, that countries are better positioned to protect their national interest. If there is one thing that has marked Latin America's position in world affairs in the new century it has been precisely this diversification of its international linkages, especially with Asia and Africa.[45]

Conclusion

As we have seen, Active Non-Alignment arose originally in 2019–20 in Latin America as the region was hit by a triple whammy: the COVID-19 pandemic, in which the region had the highest death toll in the world; the biggest economic downturn in 120 years, as regional GDP fell by 6.6 percent (the highest of any region) in 2020, a year in which global GDP fell by 3.3 percent; and inordinate pressure both from Washington and from Beijing to adopt positions on a variety of issues. In this context, ANA emerged as the best response to such a challenging international environment, and represented, as Brian Winter put it in *Foreign Affairs*, "the region's most important foreign policy development since the end of the Cold War."[46]

Yet, events in 2022–4 were to give a strong impetus to ANA beyond Latin America and across the Global South. Such was the case with the Russian invasion of Ukraine, as discussed in Chapter 1; the expansion of the BRICS group, to be analyzed in Chapter 7; and the war in Gaza, as described earlier in this chapter. Together, these developments contributed to the sudden rise of the Global South as a dynamic new force in world politics, and to its concomitant phenomenon, that of ANA. The latter, of course, does not emerge in a vacuum, but draws on a long and honorable tradition, that of non-alignment and the Non-Aligned Movement, to which we turn in Chapter 3.

3

The Cold War, Decolonization and the Non-Aligned Movement

On November 30, 1954, Marshal Josip Broz Tito, the Yugoslav leader, set off on a two-and-a-half-month-long trip to Asia in his yacht *Galeb*. The purpose of the trip was to undertake official visits to India and Burma, to meet with Tito's counterparts, prime ministers Jawaharlal Nehru and U Nu, to discuss with them the state of the world in the early years of the Cold War, and to explore the possibilities of joint action by nations not willing to align themselves with either of the two blocs, one led by the United States, the other by the Soviet Union. Tito spent a little over two weeks in India, where he visited fourteen cities as well as factories, military units and universities, and even went on a tiger-hunting safari. The substantive part of his agenda, however, was devoted to extended (often one-to-one) meetings with Nehru in New Delhi, during which they discussed the way forward for their countries in a world racked by serious tensions between the two superpowers and haunted by the specter of nuclear war.

Yugoslavia had fallen out with the Soviet Union in 1948 and was attempting to find a "third way" in that bipolar world. In turn, newly independent India was trying to find its own way in this world, even as it emerged as a leader of post-colonial states. In a speech to the Indian Parliament, Tito singled out four factors as threats to peace: a) international inequality among nations; b) the meddling of the Great Powers in the affairs of weaker states; c) the division of the world into blocs; and d) colonialism. Tito argued for keeping an equal distance between East and West, as well as for "active coexistence," and for reaching beyond passive neutralism, deploying a more pro-active stance in the resolution of international crises as well as more functional cooperation between states. A joint declaration issued on December 22 reflected the remarkable meeting of minds that took place between these two unlikely partners – Nehru, the Cambridge-educated Brahmin, and Tito, the peasant turned guerrilla fighter – as they crafted an approach that was to change the course of world politics. The document stated that "the policy of non-alignment with blocs . . . does not represent passivity as is sometimes alleged. It represents the positive, active and constructive policy that, as its goal, has collective peace as the foundation of collective security."[1]

It is difficult to overestimate the significance of this encounter between Tito and Nehru. Tito's perspective and his European background brought a universal dimension to Asian discussions on neutralism. The subsequent Bandung Conference of Afro-Asian states in 1955 suddenly acquired a fresh impetus, reaching beyond the confines of post-colonial states to a global scale, and giving what would become the Non-Aligned Movement, formally established in Belgrade in 1961, a broader and more transversal meaning.

Curiously, though, the term non-alignment itself did not feature in the debates and documents of the Bandung Conference, otherwise regarded as the birthplace of the concept. In the other landmark event in the development of the notion, the 1956 Brioni meeting between Tito, Nehru and Nasser, the term was not used either.[2]

The notion, however, is older, and goes back to the struggle for Indian independence and the towering figure of Jawaharlal

Nehru. As he put it in 1947: "We propose to stand on our own feet and cooperate with all others who are prepared to cooperate with us. We don't intend to be the plaything of others."[3] This was one of several statements he made in the 1940s asserting the need for a foreign policy that would not be subservient to any external power. Nehru linked it to the support for the independence of colonial peoples and the preservation of peace. In September 1946, when he was Vice Premier and Foreign Minister in the last British government in India, he declared: "In the sphere of foreign affairs, India will follow an independent policy, keeping away from the power politics of groups aligned one against another. She will uphold the principle of freedom for dependent peoples and will oppose racial discrimination wheresoever it may occur."[4] And later, in 1949 when he was Prime Minister of India: "We would better serve the cause of peace if we could pursue an independent policy friendly to other countries, but, nevertheless, independent, then if we were tied down to the policies of other nations. Our policy of non-alignment remains as it was."[5] Nehru was addressing the two main challenges faced by the international system in the post-war period: the emergence of the Cold War, and decolonization.

Roots and branches

The Cold War – the struggle, short of armed confrontation, between the United States and the Union of Soviet Socialist Republics to consolidate and extend their spheres of influence – began shortly after the end of World War II. The years 1948–50 saw the Soviet blockade of West Berlin, the creation of NATO as an anti-Soviet military alliance, the explosion of the first Soviet atomic bomb, the victory of the communist revolution in China and the Soviet-supported invasion of South Korea by North Korea. This period also saw the rift between the Soviet Union and Yugoslavia resulting from Tito's attempt at asserting autonomy. After a heated exchange of letters between him and Stalin, Yugoslavia ceased to be a member of the Soviet bloc in June 1948.

US/USSR tensions subsided somewhat in the mid-1950s, particularly after the 1956 20th Congress of the Communist Party of the Soviet Union (CPSU) in which Khruschev denounced Stalin's personality cult. The founding of the Warsaw Pact as a Soviet-bloc military alliance to counter NATO simply recognized the existing status quo. The conflict flared up again in the 1960s, with the Berlin Crisis of 1961, the Cuban Missile Crisis of 1962 and the beginning of the Vietnam War in 1964.

Coexisting and interacting with the Cold War was decolonization, beginning in Asia in 1945–9 with Indonesia, Korea, Vietnam, Jordan, Philippines, Syria, India, Pakistan, Burma and Ceylon. This was followed in the 1950s by a further twelve countries, in Asia (Cambodia and Malaysia), the Maghreb (Libya, Morocco, Tunisia) and Sub-Saharan Africa (Sudan, Ghana, Upper Volta/Burkina Faso, Central African Republic, Chad, Congo and Guinea), and in the 1960s by thirty-nine other countries, mostly in Africa and in the Caribbean.

These were the countries that gave rise to the Non-Aligned Movement. It was by no means a politically homogeneous group. In it were self-proclaimed communist countries such as North Vietnam, as well as staunch anti-communist ones like the Philippines. Many were closer to the United States and the West (e.g. Ceylon, Jordan, Pakistan, Thailand), while others had economic and even military ties with the Soviet bloc, such as Indonesia, Burma, Cambodia and Syria. Their common denominator was the belief that the Cold War posed a danger to their national prospects and progress, and that they should therefore not be involved in it but focus on strengthening world peace instead.

The first expression of this was the notion of peaceful coexistence, initially articulated in the bilateral negotiations between India and China concerning Tibet. In April 1954 the two countries signed an Agreement between the Republic of India and the People's Republic of China on Trade and Intercourse between Tibet Region of China and India. The first paragraph of the Preamble of the Agreement enumerated five principles on which relations between the two countries should be based; they were named *Panchsheel* after the old Sanskrit word *pancasila*, meaning "five precepts." They are:

1. mutual respect for each other's territorial integrity and sovereignty,
2. mutual non-aggression,
3. mutual non-interference in each other's internal affairs,
4. equality and mutual benefit, and
5. peaceful co-existence.[6]

The five points were reaffirmed in a joint statement by Nehru and Zhou Enlai issued at the end of talks held in New Delhi in June 1954. The statement further pointed out that "if these principles are applied . . . in international relations generally, they would form a solid foundation for peace and security." Recognizing that "different social and political systems exist in various parts of Asia and the world," the statement nonetheless insisted that if "the above-mentioned principles are accepted and acted upon and there is no interference by any one country with another, these differences should not come in the way of peace or create conflicts."[7]

Enter Tito

Two major developments in the early 1950s were the incorporation of Yugoslavia into the budding non-alignment group and the revolutionary *coup d'état* in Egypt that overthrew the monarchy and brought to power the nationalist military government headed initially by General Mohamed Naguib and later by Gamal Abdel Nasser.

In the case of Yugoslavia, after the split with the Soviet Union in 1948 the country found itself isolated and in need of support. For this, President Tito turned to the United States. US-Yugoslavia agreements on economic and military assistance and economic cooperation were concluded in 1951–2, and in 1953 an Agreement of Friendship and Cooperation was signed with Greece and Turkey (the Balkan Pact). As both of these countries were members of NATO, the Pact entailed an indirect association with the latter. At the same time, however, Tito as a socialist leader did not want to appear to be too close to the Western bloc. He thus pursued an independent line in the United Nations.

The first expression of this approach was Yugoslavia's vote on UNGA Resolution 376 (V) in October 1950 authorizing UN troops deployed in Korea to cross the 38th Parallel into North Korea. This matter was within the purview of the Security Council, but because of the Soviet veto the US took it to the UNGA, where it could muster the votes. The resolution was adopted with forty-seven votes in favor, five against (the Soviet bloc) and seven abstentions: Egypt, India, Lebanon, Saudi Arabia, Syria, Yemen and Yugoslavia. In this period, Yugoslavia intensified its contacts in New York with the representatives of India and Egypt in the UN Security Council, as well as with other former colonial countries, on issues related to anti-colonialism, collective security and economic cooperation. In late 1952, Yugoslav diplomats received instructions to develop contacts with the representatives of African and Asian countries. The Yugoslav press also published a series of articles about the problems of anti-colonial policy and development in the newly independent African and Asian countries.[8]

As mentioned above, a decisive further development was Tito's visit to India and Burma in 1954–5. Nehru was impressed with Yugoslavia breaking out of the Soviet bloc, while Yugoslavia had had close relations with Burma since the 1940s, including in the military field.[9]

Tito and Nehru met in Delhi in December 1954 and issued a joint statement which reiterated the Panchsheel principles but went beyond the language currently in use at the time by referring to "the policy of non-alignment adopted and pursued by their respective countries." Crucially it also added a new element. Tito proposed that, in the description of the policy in the original draft ("the policy . . . is not 'neutrality' or 'neutralism' and therefore passivity as sometimes alleged but is a positive and constructive policy seeking to lead to a collective peace"), the word "active" be inserted between "positive" and "constructive."

Nehru was initially "hesitant" about Tito's proposal.[10] This is odd, as Nehru had been internationally active in 1950 leading a peace initiative in the Korean conflict. Yet, since that initiative failed, this might have given Nehru reason to pause. Perhaps more relevant is the fact that in the 1930s, Nehru – after, again, some initial hesitation – had become an enthusiastic supporter of Ghandi's *satyagraha* (loosely translated as "the force of truth"), the movement of passive resistance originally deployed against the British salt monopoly.[11] In the event, Nehru agreed to Tito's proposal and the word was inserted, becoming subsequently common usage in the expression "active peaceful coexistence."[12]

The second new element in the joint statement is the rejection of the notion that there is a "third bloc" or "third force" of non-aligned countries. This conception is "repudiated" as "a contradiction in terms because such a bloc would involve them in the very system of alignments which they regard as undesirable." This view has continued to dominate the NAM, which as a result has never had a permanent secretariat. A proposal to set one up was rejected by a large majority at the first meeting of heads of state that took place in Belgrade in 1961 and has not been revived since.

The Panchsheel principles would form the basis for the main outcome of the Bandung Conference, and were later proclaimed, in a slightly modified wording, by the UNGA as a means "to develop friendly and co-operative relations and settle disputes by peaceful means."[13]

Birthplace Bandung

The next major milestone was the Bandung Conference.[14] It was convened by the prime ministers of Burma, Ceylon, India, Indonesia and Pakistan as an Asian-African gathering to promote goodwill and cooperation among the nations of Asia and Africa. It aimed to consider social, economic and cultural problems – in particular issues around national sovereignty, racialism and colonialism – and the position of Asia and Africa and their peoples in the world and the contribution they could make to the promotion of world peace and cooperation.[15]

The conference took place from April 18–24, 1955 in Bandung, Indonesia, and was attended by twenty-nine countries: Afghanistan, Burma, Cambodia, Ceylon, the People's Republic of China, Egypt, Ethiopia, the Gold Coast, India, Indonesia, Iran, Iraq, Japan, Jordan, Laos, Lebanon, Liberia, Libya, Nepal, Pakistan, Philippines, Saudi Arabia, Sudan, Syria, Thailand, Turkey, the Democratic Republic of Vietnam, the State of Vietnam and Yemen.

Items on which there was agreement were: support for peaceful coexistence and the Panchsheel principles; the rejection of colonialism; support for the Palestinian cause; and support for disarmament. The main bone of contention was communism. While some countries (e.g. Cambodia) saw the conference as a possible instrument to bridge the gap between communism and anti-communism, others denounced communism. The statement by Muhammad Fadhil Jamali, head of the Iraqi delegation, was the most vigorous of the denunciations:

> International forces now prevent peace and harmony and must be fought with determination. [One such is] communism, atheistic and materialist. It is a subversive religion, breeding hatred. The newly freed peoples of Asia and Africa are in danger of falling out of the frying pan into the fire. The communist leaders seek territorial gain . . . Under the communist domination all is silence. We must therefore defend ourselves pending an ideological disarmament throughout the world. May this conference be a step towards that essential end.[16]

Anti-communist speeches were also delivered by Pakistan's Prime Minister Mohammed Ali, the Philippines' Carlos Romulo, and Thailand's Foreign Minister Prince Wan Waithayakon. Ceylon's Prime Minister, Sir John Kotelawala, who in his opening speech had said Asia and Africa could offer themselves as "mediators in the dispute between the giants of Communism and anti-Communism,"[17] nevertheless strongly supported a proposal from Jamali to expand the notion of colonialism to cover not only that of the West in Asia and Africa but also the Soviet satellites in Eastern Europe. This was objected to by Nehru and Zhou, but the motion carried, and the final declaration condemned "colonialism in all its manifestations."[18] Zhou, who had declined to deliver an opening speech, having circulated a mimeographed text beforehand, changed his mind following the anti-communist barrage, and took the floor. His reply was unexpectedly mild and conciliatory:

> The Chinese Delegation has come here to seek unity and not to quarrel. We Communists do not hide the fact that we believe in communism and that we consider the socialist system a good system. There is no need at this Conference to publicize one's ideology and the political system of one's country, although differences do exist among us.
>
> The Chinese Delegation has come here to seek common ground, and not to create divergence . . . The overwhelming

> majority of the Asian and African countries and peoples have suffered and are still suffering from the calamities under colonialism. . . . If we seek common ground in doing away with the sufferings and calamities under colonialism, it will be very easy for us to have mutual understanding and respect, mutual sympathy and support.[19]

In spite of the differences, the Bandung Conference was able to agree unanimously on the text of a communiqué that covered economic cooperation to meet "the urgency of promoting economic development in the Asian-African region"; cultural cooperation; human rights and self-determination; colonialism, which in all its manifestations was declared an evil that should speedily be brought to an end; support for the rights of the Arab people of Palestine, the implementation of the UN resolutions on Palestine and the achievement of a peaceful settlement of the Palestine question; and the promotion of world peace and cooperation, with all nations having the right freely to choose their own political and economic systems and their own way of life.

The conference agreed that, to achieve these goals, international relations and interactions should be based on ten fundamental principles. These included the five Panchsheel precepts, in slightly modified language, together with references to fundamental human rights, equality of races and nations, the right to self-defense, exclusion of pressures on other countries and "respect for justice and international obligations" – the latter phrase a concession to the more conservative participants who did not want a radical break with the colonial powers.[20]

Encounter in Brioni

The Bandung Conference was a momentous development in the post-war scene. But the group was too heterogeneous to undertake regular, coherent activities. Nehru was aware of this, and his preference was for a looser, multipronged strategy aimed at promoting direct dialogue between the superpowers. Tito, on the other hand, felt that closer coordination was both feasible and desirable, and he found a receptive ear in Nasser.

A first expression of this was Tito's invitation to the other two leaders to a meeting at his Brioni summer residence in July 1956. The purpose was to develop the policy guidelines agreed at Bandung. The statement on the meeting reaffirmed the leaders' adherence to the principles of peaceful and active coexistence, in particular the ten Bandung principles, and identified disarmament and development as priority areas for international action. They stressed the importance of international economic and financial cooperation and called for the removal of embargoes and obstacles to the normal flow of international trade, issues that resonate to this day.

The statement identified three areas of the world where tensions could lead to open conflict (Central Europe, the Far East and the Middle East), and proposed possible solutions, including a dialogue on the future of Germany and on China's return to the UNSC. On the Middle East, the statement reads: "the conflicting interests of great powers have added to the difficulty of the situation. These problems should be considered on their merits, safeguarding legitimate economic interests, but basing solutions on the freedom of the people concerned." Strong support is expressed for Palestine and for Algerian independence.

In the words of two perceptive students of the NAM, the future shape of the movement "was clearly visible at this summit, which emphasized collective security, peaceful and active coexistence, political and economic independence, disassociation from bloc divisions, concrete economic assistance to developing countries, and negotiated solutions for current international problems as a guarantee of world peace."[21]

The response of the West to the Brioni statement was largely positive, reflecting relief at its moderate tone, in particular the reference to protecting "legitimate economic interests."

On the other hand, strong support came quickly from other major non-aligned countries. The day after the meeting, Cambodia's Norodom Sihanouk, who was on an official visit to Yugoslavia, fully endorsed the Brioni statement, and two months later Indonesia's Sukarno did likewise.

This encouraged Tito. His next step was an invitation to four leaders of non-aligned countries to propose a UN resolution urging the superpowers to resume peace negotiations. In September 1960 a meeting took place in the Yugoslav mission in New York, attended by Nehru, Sukarno, Nasser, Tito and Ghana's Kwame Nkrumah – a remarkable group in so many ways.

Nehru and Nkrumah were the intellectuals: Nehru, the oldest of the group, member of a Kashmiri Brahmin family and a Cambridge graduate, a master of the English language who had written extensive historical treatises while languishing in British prisons in India, penalized for leading the independence movement; Nkrumah, a philosophy student and later lecturer for ten years in the US and London, before returning to lead the independence movement in what would become Ghana; Tito, the anti-Nazi partisan leader of peasant stock, three years younger than Nehru, a self-taught military strategist, communist revolutionary and consummate politician, who succeeded in uniting all the South Slavic peoples – except the Bulgarians – to create Yugoslavia; Sukarno, a successful architect turned political activist and communitarian socialist, who went on to lead the Indonesian struggle for independence from the Netherlands; and finally the youngest, Nasser, the radical Pan-Arab nationalist who inherited from his father a deep pride in the "glory of the Arabs."[22]

The meeting produced a joint resolution that was put to the UNGA. In the event, the resolution was not carried, but it received a great deal of attention, including in the international media. A year later, the first conference of the heads of state of non-aligned countries was held in Belgrade, sponsored by Tito and Nasser, who sent separate letters to the leaders of the twenty-one non-aligned countries, inviting them to a preparatory meeting in Cairo. Nehru was still doubtful, but went along. Sukarno, who was promoting, together with China, the idea of a second Bandung Conference, also supported Tito's and Nasser's initiative. India subsequently became one of the co-sponsors.

Belgrade as the launching pad

The first Summit Conference of Heads of State or Government of the NAM took place on September 1–6, 1961, in Belgrade, Yugoslavia, attended by Afghanistan, Algeria, Burma, Cambodia, Ceylon, Congo, Cuba, Cyprus, Ethiopia, Ghana, Guinea, India, Indonesia, Iraq, Lebanon, Mali, Morocco, Nepal, Saudi Arabia, Somalia, Sudan, Tunisia, United Arab Republic, Yemen and Yugoslavia, with Bolivia, Brazil and Ecuador as observers.

The conference produced the Belgrade Declaration, a document stating the essential tenets of non-alignment. Its preamble declares that "the dynamic processes and forms of social change often result in or represent a conflict between the old established and the new emerging nationalist forces," and that "a lasting peace can be achieved only if this confrontation leads to a world where the domination of colonialism-imperialism and neo-colonialism in all their manifestations is radically eliminated" and a policy of peaceful coexistence in the world is accepted and practiced.

The document goes on to proclaim the right of all nations to "unity, self-determination, and independence by virtue of which right they can determine their political status and freely pursue their economic, social cultural development without intimidation or hindrance" and "freely dispose of their natural wealth and resources without prejudice to any obligations arising out of international economic cooperation, based on the principle of mutual benefit and international law."

Disarmament is declared to be the "most urgent task of mankind" and a substantial part of the document is devoted to it, leading to a call to the Great Powers to sign without delay a treaty for general and complete disarmament. Issues of economic development are also raised, albeit with somewhat less prominence. Efforts are called for to "remove economic imbalance inherited from colonialism and imperialism and to close, through accelerated economic, industrial and agricultural development, the ever-widening gap in the standards of living between the few economically advanced countries and the many economically less-developed countries."

Developing countries are invited "to co-operate effectively in the economic and commercial fields so as to face the policies of pressure in the economic sphere, as well as the harmful results which may be created by the economic blocs of the industrial countries." They are further invited "to consider to convene, as soon as possible, an international conference to discuss common problems and to reach an agreement on the ways and means of repelling all damage which may hinder their development; and to discuss and agree upon the most effective measures to ensure the realization of their economic and social development."

The Belgrade Conference marked the formal creation of the NAM. It was not conceived as an institutional structure empowered to produce binding commitments, but as a platform for the coordination of the international action of its members, without a permanent secretariat. The highest body of the Movement is the Summit Conference of Heads of State or Government of Non-Aligned States that meets periodically, roughly every three years. There have been eighteen summits since 1961, the most recent one in January 2024 in Kampala, with the theme "Deepening Cooperation for Shared Global Affluence."

The NAM has currently 120 members, and its endurance despite the great changes undergone by the international system (notably the collapse of the Soviet bloc and the onset of globalization), and despite some major internal conflicts, is a testament to the aspiration of the Global South for a voice of its own. The most serious test of the resilience of the NAM took place at end of the 1970s. The decade had marked the rise of Cuba to a position of leadership in the Movement, dramatically bolstered by its military intervention in Angola, which was decisive in countering the support of apartheid South Africa for the Portuguese colonial regime. The 6th NAM Summit in September 1979 took place in Havana, chaired by Fidel Castro, who was by then regarded as the iconic figure of the Movement. Then came the intervention of the Soviet Union in the civil war in Afghanistan, a member of the NAM. This was rejected by the vast majority of the membership; in the UNGA vote on a resolution condemning the Soviet Union, fifty-six NAM members voted in favor and twenty-six abstained, with only nine voting against. Cuba was among those who defended the Soviet Union. As a result, Cuba lost its leading role and Castro ceased to be active in the Movement.

New actors, new agendas

The Belgrade Declaration had recommended the convening of an international conference on economic and social development. This proposal was taken up in two ways. On the one hand, a an UNGA resolution of December 1961 requested the UN Secretary-General to consult governments on the advisability of holding an international conference on international trade problems relating especially to primary commodity markets, and on a possible provisional agenda. On the other hand, a group of ten Asian and African non-aligned countries plus Yugoslavia convened a Conference on the Problems of Economic Development. The sponsoring governments were Ceylon, Ethiopia, Ghana, Guinea, India, Indonesia, Libya, Mali, Sudan, United Arab Republic and Yugoslavia. Twenty countries in total attended, of which seven were African, eight Asian, four Latin American (Bolivia, Brazil, Cuba and Mexico), plus Cyprus. In addition, five countries attended as observers (Chile, Ecuador, Singapore, Uruguay and Venezuela).

The most significant outcome of the conference was the proposal to the UN Economic and Social Council (ECOSOC) for the convening of a Conference on Trade and Development. This was approved by ECOSOC and by the General Assembly,[23] resulting in the establishment of the United Nations Conference on Trade and Development (UNCTAD), which held its first session from March 23 to June 16, 1964, in Geneva, Switzerland. During the conference the developing country participants decided to organize themselves into a group for the purpose of negotiation with both developed and socialist countries in the economic and social fields in the UN system. Thus was born the Group of 77 (from the original number of members), currently comprising 135 countries.

The G77 was particularly active in the 1970s, when developing countries argued that the international economic system was biased against them and required a profound transformation. This led to proposals for the establishment of a New International Economic Order and a Charter of Economic Rights and Duties of States. In both cases there was a major participation of Latin American countries, in contrast with their limited previous involvement in the Non-Aligned Movement. The NIEO was endorsed by the UNGA in May 1974,[24] as was the Charter of Economic Rights and Duties of States in December that year.[25]

Both initiatives involved momentous reforms to the world economic system. A prominent proposal was to reorganize the world commodity arrangements to reduce price instability by means of a Common Fund that would intervene in the markets to smooth fluctuations. The overall approach of both proposed programs entailed a strengthened role for governments and international institutions in the management of the world economy. This was rejected from the start by the developed country group, led by the US, and was superseded by the advent of globalization in the 1980s. Little of the policy proposal content of the two initiatives came into being. Exceptions are the Generalized System of Preferences, a special trade regime for the least developed countries proposed by UNCTAD and adopted by the General Agreement on Tariffs and Trade (GATT)/World Trade Organization (WTO), and the Set of Multilaterally Agreed Equitable Principles and Rules for the Control of Restrictive Business Practices agreed in UNCTAD. Yet, these arrangements are not binding.

All of this shifted the focus of international concern of developing countries from the political/strategic field (i.e. the arms race) to the economic and social field, with an emphasis on the role of developing countries in the world economy. On the other hand, it also heralded the emergence of the Global South, loosely represented by the UN Group of 77, as a main international actor, including the Latin American countries. The Movement continues to exist in a more subdued form, and in 1994 a Joint Coordinating Committee of NAM and the G77 was established in New York to concert action in the international bodies.

The new century's new context

The concept of non-alignment is a child of the Cold War and of decolonization. There is, therefore, a legitimate question about its relevance after the end of the Cold War and the completion of decolonization. That said, the current global landscape has features which are comparable to those that gave rise to non-alignment.

The conflict between the US and China is not merely an economic quarrel with trade, investment and technology components. It is a dispute for the hegemony of the globalized world, for the definition of its rules and for its management. Walter Lippmann's acute characterization of the Cold War as "a continuous, persistent pressure towards the disruption and weakening of rival influence and rival power"[26] seems equally applicable to the Great Power rivalry of today.

Consider this 2020 statement by Mike Pompeo, at the time US Secretary of State: "My goal today is to . . . detail what the China threat means for our economy, for our liberty, and indeed for the future of free democracies around the world. The ultimate ambition of China's rulers isn't to trade with the United States. It is to raid the United States."[27] A recent official US report strikes a similar note: "China is attempting to use its own and other countries' legal systems to achieve a suite of strategic and political goals . . . [as is shown by] China's undermining of international laws that thwart Beijing's objectives and China's ongoing efforts to align international law with its illiberal values."[28]

This perception has led to the geopoliticization of international economic relations, prioritizing security, defense and geostrategic aspects over economic ones. Economic policy decisions are evaluated not according to criteria of efficiency and equity, but in terms of their potential impact on the geopolitical balance.

This approach was introduced by the first Trump administration, which began to define US-China relations in trade and technology with reference to geopolitical parameters. An iconic instance is the 2019 accusation that the Chinese company Huawei, one of the world's largest suppliers of mobile network and telecommunications equipment, was including in its products "backdoors" that would enable it to carry out espionage for the Chinese government, though no evidence was supplied to support this claim. On May 15, 2019, Trump issued the Executive Order on Securing the Information and Communications Technology and Services Supply Chain, which gives the US government the power to restrict any transactions with "foreign adversaries" that involve information and communications technology. The same day, also citing violations of economic sanctions against Iran, the US Department of Commerce added Huawei and its affiliates to its Entity List under the Export Administration Regulations. This restricts US companies from doing business with Huawei without government permission. On May 19, Reuters reported that, due to these restrictions, Google had suspended Huawei's ability to use the Android operating system on its devices with licensed Google Mobile Services. The next day, it was reported that Intel, Qualcomm and Xilinx had stopped supplying components to Huawei.[29]

This approach was continued by the Biden administration, which confirmed the blacklisting of Huawei and expanded the list of blacklisted Chinese companies to thirty-six. It also took the unprecedented step of rejecting the decision of the dispute settlement organ of the WTO that declared illegal certain restrictions on imports of Chinese steel and aluminum, stating that "the United States maintains that issues of national security cannot be reviewed in WTO dispute settlement and the WTO has no authority to second-guess the ability of a WTO Member to respond to a wide-range of threats to its security. The United States will not cede decision-making over its essential security to WTO panels."[30]

Pressures have also been exerted on Latin American countries to sever links with Chinese communications companies.

On the Chinese side, there have also been instances of the use of commercial power to serve political aims. In 2020, China imposed trade sanctions on Australia, including on barley, beef, cotton, lamb, lobsters, timber and wine, as well as coal. Although the official justification included accusations of dumping as well as the discovery of bark beetles in Chinese timber imports, the measures appear to have been related to Australian Prime Minister Scott Morrison's call for an independent investigation into the origins of COVID-19.[31]

More serious are the accusations about China's military preparations and actions. A report in *The Washington Post* refers to "China's dangerous actions in the disputed South China Sea . . . Beijing appears to be engaged in deliberate acts of provocation, testing the United States and one of its chief regional allies, the Philippines."[32] The already cited US report states that "China uses the People's Liberation Army's activities and relationships with foreign militaries to promote a positive image of China as an international security partner, undermine US influence, and pursue military, foreign policy, and economic benefits," and that "the Chinese Communist Party views its military as a tool that not only serves warfighting objectives but can also influence diplomatic, economic, and security conditions in peacetime." It further adds that "the United States and China are engaged in a de facto arms competition, and the PLA is preparing for the possibility of open confrontation. If China overtakes longstanding areas of US advantage in undersea warfare and space and establishes a decisive lead in AI, the balance of power in Asia and worldwide could be dramatically altered."[33]

Bringing ideology back in

The characterization of the US-China conflict as a Second Cold War has been criticized on the grounds that there are major differences between the original Cold War and the current dispute.[34] Those differences are real. However, as Joseph Nye has remarked, if the term "refers to an intense prolonged competition, we are already in one" (he nonetheless finds the historical analogy "inapt").[35]

A central argument against the use of the Cold War concept is the alleged lack of ideological elements in the US-China dispute. While the US and the Soviet Union represented two different and incompatible visions of the world, society and the economy, the US and China today, it is argued, embody two variants of capitalism: liberal and state-led.

Yet, the US government discourse on the subject has been nothing if not ideological. At a press conference in March 2021 President Biden said:

> I truly believe we're in a moment where history is going to look back on this time as a fundamental choice that had to be made between democracies and autocracies.
>
> You know, there's a lot of autocrats in the world who think the reason why they're going to win is democracies can't reach consensus any longer; autocracies do.
>
> That's what competition between America and China and the rest of the world is all about. It's a basic question: Can democracies still deliver for their people?[36]

These remarks were made at the launch of the American Jobs Plan, an ambitious investment initiative of the Biden administration to jump start the US economy by increasing productivity and competitiveness. It was intended to demonstrate that authoritarian regimes are not more efficient than democracies at delivering economic growth and welfare.

At the end of that year, President Biden called a Summit for Democracy, described as a virtual meeting "for leaders from government, civil society, and the private sector." The aim was to explore three themes: strengthening democracy and defending it against authoritarianism; addressing and fighting corruption; and promoting respect for human rights. According to the official communiqué, the summit was attended by "more than 275 participants, representing governments, multilateral institutions, activists, journalists, parliamentarians, human rights defenders, mayors, business and labour leaders, and other actors essential to accountable, inclusive, and transparent governance and the rule of law."[37] The first theme was highlighted by President Biden in his opening address when he identified "outside pressure from autocrats" as a major challenge for democracy: "They seek to advance their own power, export and expand their influence around the world, and justify their repressive policies and practices as a more efficient way to address today's challenges."[38] A second Summit for Democracy took place in March 2023.

The summits drew criticism from the Chinese leadership. A spokesman for the Chinese Foreign Ministry declared:

> This so-called "Summit for Democracy" is against democracy in essence. More than a year ago, the US held a summit in the name of promoting democracy. The so-called "Summit for Democracy" blatantly drew an ideological line between countries and created division in the world. It was a preposterous show in violation of the spirit of democracy and exposed the US's hegemony in the guise of democracy, which has been criticized and opposed by many countries.[39]

The summit was also criticized in the West for the fact that among the invitees were iconic non-democratic politicians, such as Philippines' Rodrigo Duterte, Brazil's Jair Bolsonaro and Poland's Mateusz Morawiecki. Equally serious is the criticism of the assumption that China is bent on spreading authoritarianism based on the Chinese model to other countries, to the detriment of democracy. A study of Chinese bilateral economic links in Southeast Asia asked the question whether China favors links with countries that have similar political regimes and found that "the nature of Chinese bilateral relations with each of them is totally uncorrelated with that expectation . . . China finds it easiest to work with countries that don't share much of its political form at all."[40] The democracy/authoritarianism dichotomy turns out therefore to be a flawed approach to understanding the dynamics of the US-China conflict.

There is, however, a political economy element to the conflict. It has to do with the choice of development models and the international disciplines that impinge on that choice. The United States, with the support of the European Union, has for some time now been trying to include in international trade agreements – multilateral, regional and bilateral – clauses and obligations whose effect is to prevent departures at the national level from the model of Anglo-Saxon neoliberal capitalism favored by those countries. In the Uruguay Round of trade negotiations which led to the creation of the WTO, they succeeded in banning the use of development policy instruments, such as performance requirements for foreign investment, which had been employed extensively and successfully in the East Asia "miracle" countries. They also were able to bring the issue of intellectual property protection into the WTO disciplines, reinforcing the control of technological progress by the multinational corporations of the advanced capitalist countries.

This effort is continuing in the current discussions on the reform of the WTO and takes the form of a sustained critique of China's economic model with respect to the role of the state, industrial policies and transfer of technology requirements for foreign investment. Further restrictions are being urged.

By contrast, the Chinese position is not to put forward an alternative model, but to press for the recognition of the right of countries to choose freely their own development path. The Chinese position paper on WTO reform states: "It is imperative to respect the diversity of development models among Members and to promote fair competition in the areas of trade and investment. Such efforts would strengthen the inclusiveness of the multilateral trading system."[41]

Conclusion

The notion of non-alignment has a long and honorable history. The original formulation was tied to the context in which it emerged. Many of its features are not relevant today. Its essence, though, is as current as ever: the right of countries to decide freely their domestic and foreign policies without the constraint of alignment with the major powers. Many aspects of the original debates ring contemporary: the active character of the policy, initially put forward by Tito, and the views on neutrality and equidistance set forth by Nehru, show how visionary the founding fathers were. ANA retrieves those features, adapts them to the realities of the new century and offers the Global South a road map to navigate the turbulent waters of our time.

A key difference between the realities of the mid-twentieth century, which gave rise to the NAM, and those of the new century, which frame the choices faced by ANA, lies in the dynamics and functioning of the world economy. What are those realities and what development challenges are faced by countries in Africa, Asia and Latin America today? That is the subject of the next chapter.

4

The Political Economy of Active Non-Alignment

There is no universal theory of development. Adaptation to specific historical circumstances is key in determining its relevance. Dominant theories are the product of a certain time and place. In the 1970s, dependency theory dominated Latin American progressive thought.[1] It responded to the challenges that arose in a period of undisputed US hegemony in the region. It opened new intellectual horizons, but failed to propose alternative policies. That period is now behind us, and the balance left by decades of dependency is a negative one. Invasions, support for *coups d'état* and undue pressures on sovereign nations are part of it. In Latin America, as in Africa, no country managed to overcome the condition of underdevelopment.

In the 1980s, with the emergence of globalization, the notion arose that a fast track to development could be guaranteed with the recipes included in the Washington Consensus.[2] Freed from protectionist obstacles, the free play of market forces would be enough to keep the economies humming. Once again, expectations were thwarted. The much-heralded reforms did not produce the expected results. The relations of dependence on the hegemonic power were relaxed somewhat, but without substantially altering the pattern of international insertion subordinated to the large global production chains. Paradoxically, the progressive governments identified as part of the "Pink Wave" that held sway during the first decade of the new century ended up deepening this pattern.[3] In fact, they produced economic growth and poverty reduction by relying on the 2003–13 super-cycle of commodity prices. Instead of betting on the diversification of productive structures, they doubled down on the export of primary products. The absence of a theory with proposals leading to a development strategy became apparent.

Latin America has been especially affected by the COVID-19 pandemic and the economic crisis it caused. The Economic Commission for Latin America and the Caribbean (ECLAC) has confirmed the existence of a new "lost decade."[4] Projections for the coming years do not anticipate a change of trends towards relative stagnation.

The region needs to define a strategy that opens new perspectives. It is urgent to craft an alternative approach to deal with the new international scenario. The latter is characterized by a hegemonic dispute radically different from that of the previous period, but one that offers significant opportunities for developing nations.

The fragmentation of hegemony

Hand in hand with the rise of neoliberalism, in the 1980s a certain economic paradigm came to the fore. It was based on the transition from an international economy to a truly global one.[5] This is not a purely semantic distinction. In the international economy, nations, states and governments are key actors. Economic activity takes place mainly within national borders and the conditions of production and consumption have distinctive national features that companies must respect.

International trade is based on exchanges between nations and productive relocation is still embryonic.

The global economy, in contrast, arises as an increasingly homogeneous space where national borders become less relevant. Similar conditions of production and consumption spread around the world. The same companies, increasingly disconnected from their national origins, produce in different locations depending on the size of the internal market, the cost of labor, proximity to large markets or the availability of natural resources. Economic logic is predominant. Productive activities are relocated from the nations of origin of the companies (which become multinational or transnational) to places that offer comparative advantages in various areas. Goods and services flow through internal company channels, ceasing to be exchanges between nations and becoming intra-company transfers. National laws and regulations lose significance, as states find themselves increasingly powerless to regulate and guide economic processes. The logic is that of an international division of labor organized according to the decisions of large corporations, which limits the scope of competition and the effects of national economic policies. The turnover of major global corporations exceeds the GDP of most nations.

This was the dominant paradigm at the beginning of the 2000s. There were great national disparities and many obstacles to the free mobility of factors, but the trend was unmistakable. It pointed to a world transformed into a large, homogeneous space, organized by big multinational companies that imposed their rationality on the entire planet. This is how global value chains and factories were organized to maximize the most efficient use of available factors and conditions. This imposition of common production and consumption standards, both more competitive and more attractive, displaced the established national ones.

The fall of the Berlin Wall and the dissolution of the Soviet Union was a milestone in this process. The disappearance of the socialist camp was interpreted as the undisputed triumph of capitalism. The mantra became that globalization was unstoppable, and that hyper-globalization and the end of history followed from it.[6]

This somewhat naive neoliberal vision is now in question. What is taking place is not deglobalization, as some have prematurely predicted, but the abrupt end of hyper-globalization as it had developed during the last decades.[7] The COVID-19 pandemic and the war caused by Russia's invasion of Ukraine have played a key role in this, but there were preceding factors.

An important antecedent was the paralysis of the World Trade Organization, created in 1995 to replace the General Agreement on Tariffs and Trade. This paralysis resulted from the failure of the Doha Round that began in 2001, which sought to promote greater trade liberalization. In turn, the international financial crisis triggered by the bankruptcy of Lehman Brothers in 2008 reflected the imbalances inherent in a financial globalization that had become detached from the productive sphere. The uncontrolled expansion of credit through subprime mortgages led Lehman to insolvency. A financial panic was unleashed, forcing an emergency intervention by the Federal Reserve and the ensuing international financial crisis, the most significant since the Great Depression.

Another important factor in this was the escalation of the dispute between China and the United States, starting in March 2018 under the first Trump administration. The imposition of tariffs of $50 billion on Chinese products under Article 301 of the US Trade Law led to a true trade war that sharpened the rivalry between the two superpowers. Although the escalation was contained, President Biden's new administration kept the tariffs. This event marked the beginning of the era of neo-mercantilist industrial policies in the US.[8]

Two macro events added fuel to the fire of what *The Economist* has referred to as "slowbalization": the COVID-19 pandemic, on the one hand, and the invasion of Ukraine by

Russia, on the other. The pandemic highlighted the risks that high levels of dependence on imported inputs represented. Expeditious access to masks, respirators and vaccines became an issue of strategic importance. The notion of *health sovereignty*, once deemed obsolete, returned with a vengeance. Delays in supply, bottlenecks at ports and arbitrary decisions based on political criteria forced a redefinition of old approaches. In many countries, governments were forced to drastically reduce external dependence on imported inputs and implement programs to strengthen endogenous capacity.

In Europe, Russia's invasion of Ukraine unleashed the bloodiest conflict in Europe since World War II. *Friendshoring* was added to the *nearshoring* localization strategy pushed by the pandemic.[9] This meant cutting back exchanges with countries with fewer political or ideological affinities, and redirecting them towards others that are closer and more dependable. The challenges that dependence on gas from Russia created for Western Europe also highlighted the significance of *energy autonomy*. Likewise, shortages of fertilizers traditionally imported from Ukraine and Russia have caused serious disruptions to food production and exports. The old notion of *food sovereignty* also came back to the fore.[10]

In this setting, geopolitics trumps economic rationality. That the cost and price of a good produced in a certain country are lower is no longer enough of a reason to decide to buy it. Geographic proximity, but also political proximity, are as important as price. These new trends are leading to a fragmentation of the world economy. Regional blocs gain significance as subspaces that offer greater stability and security to exchanges. The open regionalism of yesteryear gives way to inward-looking blocs.

In such a scenario, a drastic readjustment of strategies and policies arises. Policies premised on the notion that openness to the world economy almost automatically has virtuous effects on the specialization of productive structures lose their relevance. States have regained prominence. They have done so not necessarily in an entrepreneurial function, but as creators of conditions that encourage innovation and productive diversification, enhance public-private alliances, and prioritize foresight and the building of alternative scenarios. All of this allows public policy options to be designed in advance and reduces the risks of improvisation.[11]

From subordination to interdependence

In the period of US hegemony, dependency relations led to a subordinate insertion into the world economy (as is well described in the extensive literature on Center-Periphery relations).[12] So much so that the USSR, the other superpower in the bipolar system extant during the Cold War, ended up recognizing Latin America as part of the exclusive zone of influence of the US. As shown in the outcome of the 1962 Cuban missile crisis, the Soviet attempt to deploy nuclear weapons in Cuba generated a reaction that forced Moscow to back down. On the other hand, due to Soviet economic, financial and technological weakness, relations with the USSR were not of interest to Latin American economies. The Soviet Union's effort to expand its relations with Latin America beyond Cuba took place more on the political, cultural and even military levels – with the sale of weapons to countries such as Peru. Economic relations were always marginal.[13]

The new international scenario is different. This time, the US is challenged by a power that exhibits great economic dynamism – so much so that China is now the main trading partner of several of the largest economies in South America, a region that represents two-thirds of the Latin American population. In the previous scenario, the type of insertion into the world economy was the equivalent of a straitjacket. Countries were stuck in whatever sphere of influence they were part of.

In the new scenario of fragmented hegemony, there are fewer constraints. It is possible to move from dependence to interdependence, that is, to more balanced relationships, in which none of the parties can unilaterally exercise power. In fact, one of the side effects of the dispute for hegemony between the two superpowers is the expansion of the margins of maneuver of developing nations.

This is what we have referred to previously as "playing the field." With a bit of strategic sense, developing countries can maximize the benefits and minimize project conditionalities as they extract concessions from the competing Great Powers.

The room for maneuver in a relationship with a monopoly is close to zero. The room that exists when dealing with two oligopolies that collude to fix prices by dividing up the markets is not much greater. If they do not compete, their respective offers will not vary much. Very different is the relationship between two powers that act in the same economic space (unlike what transpired during the Cold War) but are involved in an intense dispute.

In the case of a monopoly or a concerted oligopoly, relations of dependency are imposed in such a way that it is almost impossible to escape them. The dialectic of "development of underdevelopment,"[14] characteristic of the history of a large number of Latin American countries, prevails. In contrast, in a hegemonic dispute like the current one between the US and China, it is possible to use the new spaces opened by it to move from dependence to interdependence. This would allow Latin American nations to leave behind the modalities of subordinate international insertion that keep them in their condition of underdevelopment.

The competition between the Great Powers to deploy initiatives of interest to developing countries illustrates this well. In times of dependency, what Latin America could most aspire to was an equivalent of the Alliance for Progress, launched by President Kennedy in the early 1960s.[15] The Alliance was designed to counteract communist influence in the Western Hemisphere and thus avoid "another Cuba." Its core was made up of a set of economic and technical assistance programs, not without an important reformist bent, but whose impact was limited.

In the new century, China's Belt and Road Initiative, launched in 2013, stands out.[16] This is a major foreign policy project. The initial proposal consisted of the opening of two major trade routes, one by land and the other by sea, connecting Asia with Europe and Africa. Latin America was added only later. The idea is to strengthen economic cooperation through road, rail and port infrastructure. A key component is related to global energy interconnection through a cross-border network that allows the large-scale deployment of clean energy. Its main objectives include: policy coordination; connectivity of cross-border facilities; liberalized trade; and financial integration. More than 150 countries are currently part of the BRI. In turn, the Asian Investment and Infrastructure Bank has become a key player in financing projects that are part of the BRI. Twenty-two Latin American countries have signed on to the BRI, and eight have joined the Asian Investment and Infrastructure Bank.

The US presence in Latin America declined towards the end of the last century. It was in this context that the region's rejection of the proposal for a Free Trade Area of the Americas (FTAA), which had been put forth in Miami in 1994, took place. Washington's plan was to formalize the project during the 4th Summit of the Americas held in Mar del Plata, Argentina, in 2005. Under the leadership of presidents Kirchner, Chávez and Lula da Silva, the proposal was rejected.

It took a long time for the US to resume the initiative in the hemisphere. President Biden did it with the Americas Partnership for Economic Prosperity, announced at the Summit of the Americas held in Los Angeles in 2022. Its aim is to revitalize regional economic entities, mobilize new investments and make supply chains more resilient. The creation of jobs linked to the production of clean energy is promoted to advance decarbonization and protect biodiversity. In terms of trade, the aim is to make it more sustainable and inclusive.

China's BRI has been the subject of several criticisms. The main ones point to the excessive involvement of Chinese companies, weaknesses in environmental and social governance and, in some cases, the lack of transparency. For its part, APEP is less ambitious and mobilizes far fewer resources. Due to its enormous fiscal deficit, the US's ability to finance large infrastructure projects in the manner of the BRI is much more limited.

Still, as a result of the US-China dispute, proposals that open more space for countries in the region to overcome their modalities of international insertion, traditionally subordinated to the interests of the dominant power, have emerged. By practicing a rigorous ANA, they can associate themselves with those projects that they consider to be of interest in one initiative or another. Working with the BRI does not exclude participation in projects that may arise from APEP and vice versa. This is how, for example, a country like Chile has understood it. As discussed in Chapter 2, in October–November 2023 President Gabriel Boric made official visits both to China and to the US to discuss Chile's respective participation in the BRI and in APEP.

A new intellectual climate

The intellectual climate for implementing national (or regional) development strategies has also changed positively. Various factors have converged in recent years to favor the rebirth, even in Organisation for Economic Co-operation and Development (OECD) countries, of productive development policies, formerly called industrial policies.[17] This change has resulted from frustration over the limited capacity of market policies to generate growth and new quality jobs due to geopolitical concerns about deindustrialization, global specialization models and the emergence of China as a manufacturing power. To this we should add the race unleashed by the definition of standards for the technological platforms associated with the new cycle of innovation in digital automation and connectivity. The challenges associated with climate change and the reduction of emissions have also played a role. They have added pressure for countries to deal with the energy transition, sustainable urban mobility and the circularity of production processes. Finally, trade conflicts, exacerbated by the pandemic crisis and the war between Russia and Ukraine, have revealed the vulnerabilities of global value chains, giving new impetus to efforts to localize production and development.

The notion of industrial policy, a term whose use was banned during the years in which neoliberal approaches predominated, has acquired a new impetus. The works of economists such as Rodrik, Stiglitz, Mazzucato and Chang, among others, have played a key role in this.[18]

Mazzucato has documented the importance of the role of the state in creating the financial and technological conditions that have made possible such crucial innovations in the field of microelectronics as computing, the internet and mobile telephony. Without large state investments, especially in the defense sector, these innovations would not have been possible or would have been much delayed. The role of public policies in promoting growth has thus been recognized, based on a state that plays the role of "investor of first instance" and that can also take on a more direct entrepreneurial role if necessary. Mazzucato places the theory of value at the center of economics and proposes "rethinking the role of the State, not as a repairer of market failures, but as a capable, competent and secure configurator of the market." In this way, "vertical policies are redirected from focusing on specific sectors to addressing the main challenges – climate change, the digital divide or health objectives – to which all sectors can contribute instead of just a few."[19]

That said, we should also add the success of recently industrialized countries such as the so-called "Asian Tigers" (South Korea, Taiwan, Singapore and Hong Kong), as well as the rise of China. They have given empirical validity to the effectiveness of active industrial policies, an approach that is very different from the Washington Consensus.

However, the new relevance of industrial policies should not be seen as a late vindication of the policies that predominated in Latin America for much of the second half of the twentieth century. The balance of the application of these policies in the region is not positive. On the one hand, following the end of World War II, many countries had an industrial base that made possible a deep transformation of productive structures. The implementation of the "inward growth model" aimed at import substitution allowed the creation of a group of large companies in sectors such as electricity, steel, petrochemicals and telecommunications, among others.[20] In several countries in the region, the companies that currently have the highest stock market valuation were created because of government initiatives during the peak period of these policies.

The achievements and limits of this process have been the subject of multiple studies, among which those by Raúl Prebisch, Aníbal Pinto and Celso Furtado stand out.[21] Yet, import substitution suffered from a chronic insufficiency due to its dependence on imported capital and intermediate goods. To a certain extent, this could be managed, but only until the moment when balance of payments crises led to the stagnation of the process, critically affected by hard-currency scarcities, which were its Achilles' heel. Fernando Fajnzylber opened an important line of new research based on his analysis of the proposals for a “productive transformation” that have influenced the work of ECLAC until now.[22]

There is room, therefore, for a critical assessment of this form of industrialization, very different from that carried out in more recent periods by the countries of Southeast and East Asia. In Latin America, industrialization gave rise to a set of inefficient oligopolies that survived due to the high tariff barriers that protected them from external competition. The inward growth model was not capable of promoting competitive industries that could take on international markets and thus provide much needed foreign exchange. In Southeast Asia, as in the case of the “Asian Tigers,” industrial policies were always associated with the export imperative, producing very different results.

The new industrial policies do not authorize states to promote any type of activity simply according to the preferences of the government in power. Nor are they about reproducing the successful path taken by countries like South Korea, which in a very short time has been able to develop industries that compete successfully in high-tech sectors. The case of Samsung is emblematic in this regard. This gigantic *chaebol* evolved from a modest grocery store in 1938, to a textile factory, to become today a giant in electronics, semiconductors, information technology, genetic engineering, nanotechnology and even the aerospace industry. Yet, what South Korea did in the 1970s and 1980s is simply not possible today, among other things because it is not allowed by international trade regulations that ban the sort of export subsidies that were allowed then.

To be successful, the new industrial policies must keep in mind the limits imposed and the possibilities created by four types of parameters: i) climate change and emissions reduction; ii) manufacturing digitalization or Industry 4.0; iii) new autonomies and shortening chains; and iv) social inclusion. Industrial policies are not only intended to improve productivity but must also contribute to environmental objectives. In this sense, states play a key role in financing investments, coordinating actors for decarbonization and guaranteeing that the costs and benefits of the green transition are distributed equitably. Thus, the new industrial policy promotes the transition towards e-mobility, favors the generation of electrical energy from non-conventional renewable sources and encourages recycling and the circular economy. Sustainable mobility, the energy transition and the circular economy can thus contribute to the reduction of carbon emissions.

These four coordinates define a variety of possibilities. Alternatives that reach beyond the latter will not be sustainable, whether for environmental and social reasons or due to technological obsolescence, poor competitiveness or geopolitical factors. For Mazzucato, this is not about "picking winners" in sectors or technologies that should be supported. Rather, it is about implementing "missions" in which various sectors can participate, interacting with companies of different nationalities and targeting markets without references to ideology. To achieve this, the practice of a rigorous policy of ANA constitutes an essential condition, allowing policymakers to maximize extant possibilities.

This new notion of industrial strategy thus operates in a very different context from that of the old industrialization in the era dominated by relations of dependency. The new approach expands the battery of government tools and enables the crafting of more balanced and consistent public-private alliances. This requires a redesign of the institutions in charge of guiding the processes of productive transformation, as well as public companies and banks that are well-aligned with the missions and their respective challenges. Unlike previous periods, when the definition of strategic objectives was made unilaterally by the state, now it is up to the state to create the *conditions* that facilitate the definition of missions agreed upon jointly with social actors. This is also a necessary condition to ensure the persistence of these policies over time, beyond the ideological affinities of the governments in power.

Energy transition and e-mobility

The notion of development was traditionally associated with industrialization. In this view, countries that industrialized would grow and prosper. In turn, agrarian societies would stagnate and remain backward. The Latin American experience questions this somewhat simplistic notion. After the Great Depression, many countries in the region, especially the largest ones, began to industrialize by way of import substitution. This gained momentum after the end of World War II. The so-called inward-oriented development model became the dominant paradigm. Yet, in the 1960s its limitations surfaced. Truncated industrialization became dependent on imports of intermediate and capital goods. The external sector became an insurmountable obstacle, the result of the lack of international competitiveness of local manufactured products.

Today, a new paradigm holds sway. The fight against climate change requires a profound transformation of production and consumption. The energy and transport sectors are undergoing radical changes. One fifth of total greenhouse gas emissions originates in transportation, and 40 percent of that total comes from private automobiles. Given regulation and production changes, by 2035 electric vehicles should outnumber those with combustion engines. The transition towards e-mobility is under way.

The sheer magnitude of the business is gigantic. Large automobile manufacturers seek to position themselves in this race. Whoever manages to impose its technology, will win. The transition to e-mobility goes together with the speeding up of the energy transition. Today, green manufacturing – the production of turbines, solar panels and wind power – is highly concentrated in China. Reacting to this, the US has allocated 41 percent of the Inflation Reduction Act (IRA) budget in credits to stimulate the production of clean electricity, which amounts to $161 billion.[23]

A central component of this industrial and technological dispute is access to critical raw materials. Due to its ability to conserve energy, lithium is of strategic importance. South America is home to the so-called "lithium triangle" that includes Argentina, Bolivia and Chile. It represents 53 percent of the total world reserves of that mineral. Copper also plays a critical role in the energy transition, due to its capacity to relay electricity. Chile and Peru are large producers of copper, hosting 32 percent of world reserves. Many countries in the region are making progress in the decarbonization of their energy matrixes, thanks to the introduction of non-conventional renewable energies. For Latin America, the conditions to play a relevant role in the green hydrogen industry – for many the energy of the future – are very much in place.

These changes open new opportunities for countries that have a significant endowment of critical natural resources. However, this will depend on their willingness to make a push for development and on the strategies adopted to take advantage of this opportunity. A passive attitude will lead to reproducing the old forms of dependent development, as a mere supplier of raw materials to the Center. In turn, an active strategy may facilitate a higher quality connection with international value chains. In this field, China occupies a very prominent position, but the US is making headway as well. Albemarle, the main lithium producing company in the world, is based in the US.

How developing nations position themselves in relation to each of the Great Powers in this dispute is vital. Alignment with either of them would lead to a subordinate role, with limited options. On the contrary, ANA makes it possible to take advantage of Great Power competition to increase policy options and margins of maneuver. This is what "playing the field," as discussed in Chapter 2, is all about, in today's international environment.

Chilean policy towards lithium is a relevant example. The industry is dominated by two companies, Albemarle and SQM. They work with Special Operation Contracts, since, according to the Constitution, the state owns all lithium deposits in the national territory. The state authorizes production quotas. The contracts require companies to allocate 25 percent of production for greater elaboration. This mechanism, which operates via bidding, has allowed the entry of Tsinghan, a Chinese business group specializing in the steel industry, which has ventured into the lithium industry in Argentina and Chile. The business base is thus diversified, and Chile can improve its position in the value chain through the production of lithium cathodes.

To continue moving up the value chain, the establishment of broader alliances is crucial. In the case of Chile and South America, coordination with Brazil is essential. Brazil is the South American country with the largest industrial capacity. In this context, the transition towards e-mobility offers a prime opportunity. A South American program to build electric buses for public transport – a business currently dominated by highly polluting oil buses – is one of them. It is estimated that there are around 100,000 buses in service in the main cities of South America. Their replacement by electric buses represents a huge market.

To move in this direction, a broader regional agreement is essential. This must be part of the effort to relaunch regional integration according to these new realities. The Brasília Consensus,[24] formalized in May 2023 by the twelve South American countries, constitutes a first step in that direction, including as it does the integration of production among its objectives. For regional integration to proceed, it is essential that, beyond the ideologies of the governments of the day, countries prioritize their own interests and those of the region, above and beyond external pressures. For this purpose, ANA offers a suitable conceptual framework as well as a guide to action.

Towards monetary pluralism

A political economy that responds to the current situation must deal with different issue areas. The financial architecture of the current international order is in question. The institutions that emerged from the Bretton Woods agreements do not account for the new international reality. The hegemony of the dollar is not functional in a world which includes a country like today's China. China not only questions the industrial and technological leadership of the US, but has also become the leading trading nation, and one whose GDP at purchasing power parity is higher than that of the United States.

The current international financial architecture is unable to deal with the plethora of global challenges faced by the world today. Preliminary assessments indicate that the United Nations Sustainable Development Goals, agreed on for 2030, will not be met. The recovery of post-pandemic growth, the energy transition and the closing of social and basic infrastructure gaps require a level of financial resources that institutions like the World Bank and the International Monetary Fund are unable to provide.

The diagnosis of this problem is not new. It goes back to the mid-1970s. However, efforts to move towards a new order and a new international financial architecture have not succeeded. Until now, no one has been able to drive such a change. The USSR was not in a position to do so, and was never really interested in entering into such a dispute with the US. In fact, Moscow did not have the economic and financial means to do so.

In a context of international turbulence, the rise of the Global South could alter this. Nations with very diverse political and economic systems converge in the Global South. They are riven by important differences, but they have a common interest: moving towards an international order that accounts for the emergence of new powers and makes possible a reform of its financial architecture, adapting it to the needs of a more balanced international development.

In this sense, it is worth revisiting the great debate between John Maynard Keynes and Harry Dexter White about the financial and monetary rules to govern the world once World War II ended.[25] In that debate, Keynes, perhaps that century's leading economist, advocated the adoption of the Bancor as an international monetary unit. Its value would be established in relation to a set of basic commodities. The idea was to generate an international monetary system that would avoid large trade imbalances and allow the stabilization of exchange rates. Keynes's proposal was not defeated on its merits. Rather, the establishment of the dollar as the world's de facto international currency resulted from the sheer force with which the US emerged at the end of the war, in which its economy represented half of the world's product.

The emergence of China and the relevance that the yuan has acquired creates more favorable conditions for reform of the current monetary system. For now, the euro's role is consolidated and trade agreements have recently been signed between countries that do not rely on the dollar. The strengthening of the issuance of IMF Special Drawing Rights (SDR) also points in that direction. In South America, Brazil has insisted on establishing commercial exchanges using local currencies, without relying on the dollar.[26] These are still preliminary proposals that require a high degree of convergence and macroeconomic coordination. However, the fact that they are happening at the policy level (and not just in academic discussions) is telling.

In terms of political economy, the notion of "monetary pluralism" that these proposals entail – and that is making increasing headway as the US dollar is weaponized by Washington for geopolitical objectives – corresponds exactly to the concept of ANA. This weaponization is triggering increased pushback, as what was supposed to be a neutral, near-universal medium of exchange is deployed more and more for Western strategic and ideological objectives. Overcoming dependence on the dollar does not involve replacing it with another currency, but rather crafting a more diversified system, one in which the currencies of other relevant economies also play a role.

Conclusion

In the field of politics, ANA expands the range of possibilities for gaining greater autonomy. In economic affairs, it increases the possibilities of moving towards development. In both cases these are, however, mere *possibilities* that depend on the choices made by decision-makers, choices that maximize (or not) the options presented by the current international setting of Great Power competition.

The type of international insertion plays a crucial role in the possibilities of development. Relationships of dependency tend to morph into relationships of subordination. Self-sufficiency (let alone autarky) is not an option. On the contrary, the way forward lies in participating in exchanges and in the international division of labor, but in an *active way* that allows the constant creation of new competitive advantages.

Finally, a national will for development is key. It must manifest itself in a strategy supported by a broad and powerful social bloc in order to project it over time. An ANA policy opens significant options in this regard. However, for these possibilities to come to fruition, these options must be exercised. That is the task of national (or regional) policies.

Great Powers act according to their interests, but they do so under conditions that vary from country to country. In those countries of the Global South where a desire for autonomy and development does not exist, the dominant power will establish relations of dependency and subordination. The best examples were the so-called "banana republics" that proliferated in Central America. In those cases, the internal oligarchies were content with alliances that, in exchange for the maintenance of certain privileges, agreed to the total subordination of the nation to the interests of the dominant power. These were relationships that could be described as neo-colonial.

The case of countries in which local *bourgeoisies* were willing to promote a national development project is different. In Latin American "developmental" experiences, attempts were made to move in that direction. However, dependency relationships imposed a very limited range of possibilities for these projects to prosper. Latin American developmentalism made some progress, as in Brazil, but it failed in its attempt to reverse the relationships of dependency and subordination.

The new international scenario, with a fragmented hegemony, is more conducive to different strategies. These can allow the adoption of the best technologies, wherever they come from; insertion into the most dynamic markets; and the crafting of pragmatic alliances with companies willing to establish horizontal relationships. In short, they allow the building of relationships of *interdependence*, instead of dependence.

The internal dynamics of countries generate different types of relations with the dominant power. The contrast between the relations that China establishes in Africa and those it establishes in Asia is telling. In the case of Africa, where national states tend to be weaker, domestic oligarchies are more easily subordinated to the interests of Chinese companies. Thus, relations of subordination are generated that do not lead to endogenous productive capacities. Africa has become a major supplier of raw materials (oil, uranium, iron, zinc, among others) to China. Africa also represents, although to a lesser extent, an emerging market for Chinese manufacturing. Thus, a pattern of development relying on the production of a limited number of raw materials that are exchanged for manufactured products from China, much along the lines of the old Center-Periphery system, is reenacted.

The same does not happen in much of Asia, where Chinese companies must adapt to more demanding conditions arising from the presence of greater state capacity and bourgeoisies more committed to national development projects. China is currently the main trading partner of eight of the ten ASEAN members (Brunei, Cambodia, Indonesia, Laos, Malaysia, Myanmar, Philippines, Singapore, Thailand and Vietnam), the exceptions being Brunei and Laos. Since 2018, China has become the second largest investor in ASEAN. As we shall see in the next chapter, ASEAN has managed to thrive, integrating countries with very diverse political regimes, which has not been an obstacle to establishing a less asymmetric relationship with China. Faced with large countries such as Indonesia and/or strong states such as Malaysia, Vietnam and Singapore, China has established with Southeast Asian nations a very different type of relation than the one it has with African countries.

In this regard, the US experience is not substantially different. In the case of Latin America, a relationship of subordination was finally imposed. There is, however, a telling case demonstrating that this dependence can be reversed. Indeed, a good example of national will to development is represented by South Korea. At the end of the 1950s, after the war, South Korea was a poor and highly dependent country. Today, it is a country whose GDP per capita of $35,000 vastly exceeds that of Portugal (at $24,000) and Spain (at $30,000). South Korean companies compete successfully in the most dynamic and sophisticated sectors of the world economy. Internal forces were able to overcome dependence and subordination. To achieve this, South Korea did not need to break with the United States – in fact, it remains a staunch US ally. What it did was to craft and implement policies that put forward the generation of capabilities according to its own interests and not those of others.

ANA constitutes a guide for action. It creates spaces to overcome dependency and to forge options to make the great leap to development. Although it initially emerged as a Latin American proposal, it is spreading to the rest of the Global South. It makes possible the design of national or regional development strategies. It generates approaches that assert the interests of developing countries in building a political order, a trading system and a financial architecture that are compatible with the sustainable development of the planet. ANA is a foreign policy option that represents a radical change in the face of development challenges. It leaves behind the self-victimization typical of the Third World *cahiers des doléances* of yesteryear. It stresses the capacity and the right of developing countries to take their destiny in their own hands and to cease being the plaything of others.

Are there any precedents for whole regions taking up, if not ANA per se, at least roughly similar approaches to foreign policy to deal with Great Power competition? If so, how have they fared in this endeavor? Our argument is that there is such a case, and that it throws much light on how apposite and effective this approach is under such circumstances. This is the subject of the next chapter.

5

Active Non-Alignment and the ASEAN Way

In a world order in transition, references to geography as determining geopolitical choices are common. Location plays a not insignificant role in the hard choices states face as they confront the challenges of a world in turmoil. It always has. Poland's tragic history has been marked by its location between two of Europe's Great Powers – Germany and Russia, which have had their share of conflicts – and the consequent fallout on the Polish nation. The saying, "poor Mexico, so far from God and so close to the United States," attributed to former Mexican President Porfirio Díaz, speaks eloquently to the predicament of weaker states that share borders with Great Powers.

Thus, when discussing the effect of US-China tensions on Latin America, it is frequent to hear the argument that "geography cannot be ignored." By this is meant that the region's sharing the Western Hemisphere with the US should entail that, "when push comes to shove" in the differences between Washington and Beijing, Latin American countries would not have much of a choice.[1] As part of the Americas, they would inevitably have to side with the US, and their vigorous trade and investment links with China would ultimately have to give way to the broader, continental imperative. The Monroe Doctrine may not be to everybody's liking, but it is here to stay, several authors reaffirmed at the bicentennial of the latter in 2023.[2] Geography is destiny – or so the argument goes.

Now, if this were the case, the rule would presumably hold across the board – not just in the Americas, but elsewhere as well. Yet, in the case of Southeast Asia, the argument is often reversed. There, the reasoning is that *precisely* because these nations are geographically so close to China, and have historically suffered from the effects of this fate, they would see in the US a welcome actor to balance against an eventual Chinese threat, to protect their sovereignty and territorial integrity.[3] Thus the various defense agreements with the US of countries like Singapore, Thailand, Vietnam and the Philippines, and the open arms with which US Navy ships are welcomed in the subregion.

So, which is it? Is geography destiny, or is it not? What is the effect of geography on weaker post-colonial states in the Global South as they contend with Great Power competition? What margin of maneuver do they have as they are subjected to the pressures that arise from the latter? How much does geography limit their foreign policy agenda?

The purpose of this chapter is to examine the case of the Southeast Asian nations that make up the Association of Southeast Asian Nations (ASEAN), formed by Brunei-Darussalam, Cambodia, Indonesia, Laos, Malaysia, Myanmar, Philippines, Singapore, Thailand and Vietnam.

Why focus on ASEAN? The reason is straightforward. ASEAN has been described as the most successful regional integration scheme after the European Union. Though often overlooked, its performance in the new century has been nothing short of impressive, and it tells us much about how a policy of region-building combined with non-alignment can bear fruit. One example of this nimble approach is that of ASEAN's relations with China. Although ASEAN was established in 1967 as essentially an anti-communist entity designed to buttress and support the role of the United States in Southeast Asia, in the year 2000, China proposed to sign its first free trade agreement with ASEAN (interestingly, China's first FTA with an individual country would be signed with Chile in 2005). In 2000, US-ASEAN trade was $135 billion – more than three times the China-ASEAN trade of $40 billion. However, after the signing of the China-ASEAN FTA in 2001, by 2022 China-ASEAN trade had exploded to $975 billion, more than double the US-ASEAN trade of $448 billion.

Another revealing indicator of ASEAN's dynamism in the new century is to compare its economic evolution with Japan's. In 2000, Japan was the second largest economy in the world. Its GDP of $5 trillion was eight times that of the combined ASEAN GDP of $647 billion. Yet, by 2022, Japan's GDP was only 1.2 times larger than ASEAN's, and it is projected that by 2030 ASEAN's GDP will overtake that of Japan.

This chapter, then, parses the way the ASEAN member states have handled Great Power competition in general, and the current one between the US and China in particular. Following up on the question raised in Chapter 1, the first section discusses the reaction of these countries to Russia's invasion of Ukraine; the second examines the emergence of ASEAN as a key diplomatic actor in Asia and the world more generally; the third considers the notion of "ASEAN centrality," a key feature of this entity's international projection; the fourth looks at ASEAN's crafting of the Regional Comprehensive Economic Partnership (RCEP), a fifteen-member trade agreement signed in 2020, and by now the biggest such agreement anywhere; the fifth dissects in some detail how ASEAN member states have handled Great Power competition; and the sixth undertakes a comparative exercise by looking at the results of the different approaches of Southeast Asian and Latin American nations to their foreign relations in terms of their respective summits with the US. These were both held in the US within a short time span in the spring of 2022, thus allowing for an interesting case study in "controlled comparison."

ASEAN and Russia's invasion of Ukraine

On the face of it, ASEAN members were all the over the place in their reactions to what would turn out to be the biggest land war in Europe since the end of World War II. Some, like Singapore, arguably the ASEAN member with the closest relationship to the United States, voted to condemn Russia's aggression at the UNGA vote on March 2, 2022, and went along with the unilaterally proclaimed Western sanctions against Moscow, applying them *sine die*. At the other extreme, Myanmar supported Russia's attack on its neighbor, while Laos and Vietnam did not vote to condemn Russia at the March 2 vote. Indonesia, in turn, spoke against what it considered a violation of sovereignty, but did not mention Russia. In the subsequent UNGA vote in April on suspending Russia from the United Nations Human Rights Council, six ASEAN members (including Singapore) abstained, and Laos and Vietnam voted against the resolution.[4]

Yet, far from reflecting a hodgepodge of positions with little in common, these various votes express a longstanding *leitmotiv* and running thread across ASEAN's trajectory: the refusal of its member states to align themselves systematically with one or another of the Great Powers in competition. Yes, some countries (like Laos and Vietnam) have quite direct links with Russia, going back to the latter's predecessor state, the Soviet Union; while others (like Myanmar's military regime) enjoy current political support from Moscow. But while this partially accounts for their votes, the overall thrust of these countries' foreign policies is to avoid involvement in such conflicts – the notion being that nothing good can come out of them for third parties, especially for small and middle powers. In short, the preference is for non-alignment.

As we shall see in the remainder of this chapter, from ASEAN's initial establishment in 1967 – when the subregion was racked by wars and insurrections of various kinds, and the group had a strong anti-communist component – it has come a long way.[5] It eventually incorporated one-party states like Laos and Vietnam, and now represents something much closer to a non-aligned stance in foreign affairs. In part, this is the result of the need to represent the sheer variety of regime types it encompasses – from democracies to monarchies, one-party states and military dictatorships. But it also embodies a pragmatic assessment of international realities and the lessons learned after more than a half-century of existence. Throughout the Cold War, the subsequent unipolar moment and the present transition to an as yet undetermined international system – but one marked by strong Great Power competition – ASEAN has concluded that *not* getting involved in the squabbles of the latter is by far the safest and most prudent way forward. Not without reason, ASEAN has been described as the most successful regional integration scheme after the European Union.[6] As a collective, it is already the fifth largest economy in the world in terms of GDP, with $3.7 trillion in 2023, and is projected to be the fourth largest in 2030.[7]

Less remarked upon has been its extraordinary diplomatic success, which has placed it squarely at the center of world affairs – a remarkable achievement for a group of mostly small and mid-sized countries with a troubled and conflicted history, the subject to which we now turn. It is in many ways the most successful example of weak states "playing the field," that is, playing both sides against the middle in dealing with the Great Powers, and coming out stronger from it. Tellingly, it has done so both individually and collectively; that is, both in terms of the individual foreign policies of each of the member states (with some variations, obviously) and in terms of the diplomatic stances of ASEAN as such. This is especially remarkable given the fact that Southeast Asia finds itself at one of the most critical hotspots in world affairs, smack in the middle between the two Asian giants (China and India), bordering the busiest shipping lane in the world (the Malacca Straits) and the South China Sea, site of China's aggressive maritime expansion.

The improbable rise of ASEAN to its current pole position

As Kishore Mahbubani has observed, ASEAN's trajectory must be set against the background of two factors that might have seemed to be unsurmountable obstacles to any kind of progress, let alone to the institutional strength and density the group has achieved. The first is the extraordinary heterogeneity of the region – ethnic, religious, linguistic – leading it to be labeled "the Balkans of Asia," a place that not too long ago was referred to as "Indochina," a mere transit point between the two Asian giants, China and India. The second factor is the conflicts that wreaked havoc across these lands – first the US-led war in Vietnam, and later the war between China and Vietnam.[8]

Yet, despite these unpromising conditions, ASEAN managed to become a key reference point in international affairs. Its yearly summits are attended by world leaders, including the presidents of the United States, China and Russia; it has woven a rich network of overlapping regional entities, like the ASEAN + 3, the ASEAN Regional Forum (ARF), the East Asia Summit (EAS) and the ASEAN Defense Minister's Meeting Plus (ADMM+); and it has positioned itself not just as a valid and valued interlocutor with the Great Powers, but also as one providing a platform for the latter's leaders to interact with each other less obtrusively than through the tried-and-true medium of bilateral visits.

This does not mean that ASEAN has not been tested. The Asian financial crisis of 1997 – originally triggered in Thailand, but that soon encompassed much of the subregion – was one such test, but one from which it emerged stronger than before, with the establishment of a new financial mechanism, the Chiang Mai Initiative, designed to forestall future such occurrences. In hindsight, it also scored an intellectual victory of sorts over the IMF on the issue of capital controls, a subject on which Malaysian Prime Minister Mahathir Mohamad made an impassioned argument which turned out to be right.[9]

A key element in the construction of ASEAN was the development of a certain organizational and institutional culture. This meant leaving behind the culture of *konfrontasi* favored by Indonesia in the 1960s and moving instead to one of *musyawarah* and *mufakat* (consultation and consensus), as the only way to keep such a diverse group of member states together. A related factor was the willingness of Indonesia quite self-consciously *not* to throw its weight around as by far the biggest member state, a syndrome that has been the bane of entities like the Organization of American States (with the outsize role of the US) and MERCOSUR (with the outsize role of Brazil). This left space for the sort of collective action and consensus-building so critical to the establishment of durable institutions. International entities that depend too heavily on the whims of one member state tend to be more unpredictable and seen as less trustworthy than those that do not.

Alongside this there has been what we might call a "soft" approach to decision-making and the implementation of agreed-on measures, leaving sufficient leeway for member states to proceed at the pace they deem appropriate. This is "the ASEAN Way" – light on structures, rules and enforcement, heavy on cooperation and "moving forward together."[10] It is an approach so strikingly different from, say, the one followed by the European Union – heavy on highly formalized mechanisms and decision-making structures – that it might seem like a recipe for ineffectiveness. In fact, it has been anything but that, among other things because it has ensured the unity of ASEAN and made it into a credible, predictable interlocutor with outside powers. Non-alignment and ASEAN centrality have been at the core of this phenomenon.

ASEAN centrality as a driving force

This "soft, soft" approach to internal decision-making is, however, paired with a firm determination to put ASEAN in charge of regional relations. Its Charter stresses the need to "maintain the centrality and proactive role of ASEAN as the primary driving force in its relations and cooperation with its external partners in a regional architecture that is open, transparent and inclusive."[11]

The core notion here is to keep ASEAN as the hub of the various regional entities that have sprung up around it, and not let itself be sidelined by the attempts of other powers to use the "variable geometry" that emerges from those entities. This has led to a certain amount of frustration among the Great Powers, as well as among other neighboring states like Australia, but has not deterred ASEAN from staying the course. The contrast here with the Union of South American Nations (UNASUR) could not be greater. The establishment of the latter in 2008, under the leadership of Brazil and pointing to what could have been considered a more manageable group of countries confined to the South American mainland (as opposed to other groupings encompassing Latin America and the Caribbean as a whole, a total of thirty-three countries), raised many hopes. UNASUR seemed to have the potential to end once and for all the region's fragmentation and to achieve a measure of coordination and cooperation. Yet, even before the then-crop of progressive governments was displaced by a new wave of conservative regimes less committed to the cause of regional integration, the inability of those governments to agree on a new secretary-general for the organization soon paralyzed UNASUR and condemned a once-promising project to an early demise.[12]

ASEAN, on the other hand, has made a virtue of its own weakness. Located between the two "Asian giants," and capitalizing on the fact that its very weakness does not threaten anybody, it has deployed both this geographic location and its knack for collective action as key assets to enhance its own standing. This has translated into accelerated economic growth and industrialization. In the "Factory Asia" that has arisen in the new century, with China at its core, ASEAN nations have come to play a key role in the value chains that comprise modern manufacturing. This has been made possible by the working relationship they have nurtured with Beijing, while not neglecting their ties with Washington. Thus, the remarkable economic growth we have seen in recent years, especially in Vietnam, Indonesia and Singapore, but also across the region.[13]

In turn, the notion of "centrality" has facilitated the emergence of ASEAN not just as a key diplomatic interlocutor in Asia, but also as one that provides a handy platform for other powers to interact with each other – a not inconsiderable advantage. Far from having to court the Great Powers, ASEAN nations find themselves in the enviable position of being courted themselves, as we shall see below. As Amitav Acharya has put it, centrality thus had both a strategic and a normative purpose.[14] From a strategic perspective, it meant putting the entity and its member states in a key position in the post-Cold War era, in the middle of things, as a reference point for the Great Powers and other nations keen to interact with Asia, and one to be ignored at their peril. From a normative standpoint, the "ASEAN Way" of consensus-based, open regionalism embodied an attractive manner of doing business, one that could also translate into diplomatic platforms that would reflect such an approach, giving guarantees to all parties.

Yet, far from remaining content with the status quo, ASEAN has also been keen to continue to grow and enhance Asia's regional space. Thus, the Regional Comprehensive Economic Partnership.

The rise of the RCEP

The signing of the RCEP in November 2020 was widely described in Western media as a significant diplomatic victory for China.[15] A trade agreement between China, Japan, South Korea, Australia, New Zealand and all ten ASEAN members, it instantly became the largest such agreement anywhere, with a market of 2.2 billion people (30 percent of the world's population) and a GDP of a little over $26 trillion (30 percent of the global GDP). As a result of it, in a period of less than four years – and after the United States had already jettisoned the Trans-Pacific Partnership (TPP) it had so arduously fought for for nine years (ever since the George W. Bush administration) – Washington ended up ceding significant ground on the trade front in the world's fastest growing and most dynamic area, the Asia-Pacific. Yet, what was less remarked upon was the fact that the RCEP had not been a Chinese initiative, but an ASEAN one.

Though long in the making – the RCEP was originally conceived at the 2011 ASEAN Summit in Bali, Indonesia, and formally initiated as a project at the Phnom Penh, Cambodia, summit in 2012 – the message its signing sent in November 2020 was unmistakable. At the height of the worst pandemic to hit humanity in a full century, with rising tensions between the US and China, and with the EU absorbed by Brexit, the signal sent by ASEAN was loud and clear: in Asia we are keen to move forward, and we will not let ourselves be sidetracked by the petty squabbles of others. For ASEAN, the protectionism being embraced across the North Atlantic was not seen as the path of the future. Neither are ASEAN members convinced that the geopolitical differences in Asia itself – say between China and Japan and South Korea, on the one hand, or even between China and Australia, on the other – should stand in the way of more liberalized trade flows in this part of the world.[16]

Revealingly, none of these differences blocked the ultimate signing of the RCEP. A criticism of the agreement voiced by international trade specialists had to do with its limited character, namely that it basically deals with trade in goods.[17] This would make it merely what is known as a "first-generation" trade agreement, one much less ambitious than the original TPP, or even the subsequent Comprehensive and Progressive Agreement for Trans-Pacific Partnership (CPTPP), which includes extensive "beyond the border" disciplines on matters like competition, state-owned enterprises (SOEs) and government procurement, and several other such areas addressed by second- and third-generation trade agreements. Yet, the RCEP does include references to such critical matters as the regulation of carbon emissions, agricultural subsidies, intellectual property, communications and services, so it should not be underestimated. Moreover, it could well be argued that it was the "softly, softly" approach followed by ASEAN that brought such an ambitious undertaking as the RCEP to a successful conclusion. Instead of setting itself extremely ambitious (and perhaps unachievable) goals, ASEAN is willing to settle for more modest but achievable objectives, and actually reach them.

The Belt and Road Initiative and the Free and Open Indo-Pacific project

A revealing instance of how ASEAN manages its relations with the Great Powers, playing the field and hedging its bets, is that of its reaction to China's Belt and Road Initiative (BRI), on the one hand, and to the US's Free and Open Indo-Pacific (FOIP) project on the other.

The BRI is a major Chinese foreign policy initiative launched by President Xi Jinping in 2013.[18] It has since become Beijing's most significant international project in the new century. Introduced via major speeches by Xi, first in Astana and later in Jakarta, it was originally designed to connect the world's fastest growing area, East Asia, with the world's biggest market, the European Union, thus recreating Eurasia. This ambitious undertaking would proceed both by land, across Central Asia, through highways, railways, bridges and tunnels of various kinds ("the Belt"), as well by sea ("the Maritime Silk Road" – somewhat confusingly, "the Road"), across the Indian Ocean and the Red Sea, all the way to the Mediterranean. References to the Silk Road of yesteryear, once traversed by the likes of Marco Polo, aimed to give the project historical depth. Initial concerns about where the funds for such a huge project would come from, and about the institutional framework to support it, were soon dispelled with the 2015 establishment of two major multilateral development banks – the Asian Investment and Infrastructure Bank and the New Development Bank, headquartered in Beijing and in Shanghai respectively.[19]

Partly in reaction to the BRI, in 2017 the United States launched its own project for the region, known as the FOIP, first broached by President Trump at an Asia-Pacific Economic Cooperation (APEC) Summit held in Hanoi in November 2017.[20] A branding and strategic exercise rather than an economic project, it aimed to do for the vast expanses of the Pacific and Indian oceans what the BRI was doing across the Eurasian landmass. The basic underlying notion was that the longstanding denomination of that part of the world as "Asia-Pacific," which acquired renewed currency in the early 1990s with the onset of the post-Cold War era, was too closely associated with China, and that the time had come to rechristen it. In support of this, it was argued that given the confluence of the Pacific and Indian oceans, as well as the fact that the main trade routes go across both, it is only logical to consider them in an integrated fashion. It was also pointed out that the term "Indo-Pacific" has a long history, and its use today would only revive a longstanding conception that attests better to the dynamic and the functioning of the "world's maritime highway," where much of the world's trade transits, particularly across the Malacca Straits. Fragmentary perspectives that artificially split up these oceans on Asia's coasts only obscure the integrated maritime reality.[21] That said, there is little doubt that much of this exercise is designed to raise the profile of India, seen as closer to the West, in order to balance China's growing weight in Asia. In this, the Quadrilateral Security Dialogue ("the Quad"), sometimes described as an "Asian NATO," formed by the United States, Japan, India and Australia, plays a key role.[22]

Both initiatives put ASEAN and its member states on the horns of a dilemma. How to react to them without appearing to be taking sides in this unfolding Great Power competition?

In many ways, the manner in which ASEAN managed this not inconsiderable challenge illustrates its approach to its foreign relations, one that keeps very much in mind the need for non-alignment, but now in its new incarnation, both more flexible and more proactive than the NAM's. In terms of the BRI and its offer of building infrastructure and connectivity in Southeast Asia, the ASEAN countries' reaction was in keeping with the hedging approach they have traditionally followed with the big powers in order to avoid risks, polarization and being marginalized (which is such a defining feature of ANA, as discussed in Chapter 2).[23] On the one hand, they were happy to explore the opportunity the BRI entailed in terms of improving their railway lines, highways and ports – which, given the global value chains that connect them with "Factory China" (and with the rest of the world), are critical for their international competitiveness. On the other hand, they were by no means prepared to act simply as cheerleaders for Beijing in this venture.[24] The various railway projects in the subregion illustrate this well. They also reflect the relative bargaining position of each of the ASEAN members.[25]

The case of Indonesia is an especially interesting one. The election of President Joko Widodo, the former mayor of Jakarta, in 2014, shortly after the announcement of the BRI by President Xi, brought in a government determined to make infrastructure-building a signature feature of its policies. This meshed nicely with the BRI. In this context, given China's "railway diplomacy" (i.e., its attempts to place abroad its high-speed trains, for which China has the most advanced technology), the possibility of a Chinese-built high-speed line from Jakarta to Bandung loomed large. This had the added luster of the symbolic value of Bandung as the site of the legendary 1955 conference that gave rise to the NAM. Yet, far from simply buying into the Chinese offer to proceed with the project, Indonesia drove a hard bargain, playing off China against Japan, whose companies were also interested in the project. Thus, Jakarta ended up with a much better deal.[26] In a revealing coincidence, within a few weeks of the inauguration of the Chinese-built $7.6 billion high-speed railway from Jakarta to Bandung in early September 2023, the British government announced the cancellation of the HS2 high-speed railway project to Manchester, a much-touted and longstanding project of several Tory governments, from whose tender Chinese companies had been expressly banned.

Malaysia also struck a hard bargain with China. One of the first things the newly elected government of Prime Minister Mahathir Mohamad did in 2018 was to cancel another major

Chinese railway project, deeming it too expensive – although it was ultimately restored after a visit by Mohamad to Beijing, in which the terms were renegotiated.[27] It should also be noted that perhaps the biggest beneficiary of Chinese "railway diplomacy" in Southeast Asia has been one of the poorest ASEAN members, namely Laos. There, a Chinese-built $5.6 billion railway line was inaugurated in December 2021, linking the capital, Vientiane, with Kunming in China's Yunnan province, thus ending the country's landlocked condition and connecting it to the wider world. A measure of the magnitude of the Laos railway project can be gauged from the fact that the terrain it traverses is so difficult that three fourths of the 1035 km line is made up of bridges and tunnels.[28] Throughout this process, however, ASEAN was careful not to appear to be providing a blanket endorsement of China's foreign policy in general or of the BRI in particular.

In turn, the FOIP project presented in some ways an even bigger challenge to ASEAN than the BRI. The project was promoted with great verve by Washington: in October 2020 Secretary of State Mike Pompeo made his first visit to Asia in a year to attend a meeting of Quad foreign ministers in Tokyo; President Biden hosted the first Quad Summit in the White House in March 2021; and the traditional US Pacific Command headquartered in Honolulu was renamed the "Indo-Pacific Command."[29] The BRI is ultimately about development, and it is not too difficult for developing nations to justify an association with it without necessarily being accused of "tilting" towards Beijing. As previously discussed, weaker states are primarily driven by their development concerns, something that the BRI addresses quite explicitly.

The FOIP in contrast, with its strong military and overtly ideological component, falls into an altogether different category. Moreover, by associating one of the Great Powers with three states on the periphery of Southeast Asia, and making clear that a key objective is to hinder China's expansion in the South China Sea, the FOIP managed both to question ASEAN centrality in regional affairs and to position itself squarely against China. This put ASEAN, which is not in favor of militarizing regional structures, in a difficult position. Not surprisingly, in 2018 the Chinese Foreign Minister Wang Yi referred to the very notion of the "Indo-Pacific" as a "headline grabbing" idea that will "dissipate like sea foam."[30]

Doing nothing, and pretending the FOIP could be ignored, was always an option, but that is not the ASEAN Way. Reflecting its proactive approach, in 2019 it produced a document on the FOIP, entitled "ASEAN Outlook on the Indo-Pacific," taking note of these new developments.[31] The text acknowledges that the notion of the Indo-Pacific has resonated (a measure of this is that even Germany, of all countries, and whose relation with the region is, at best, tenuous, released a document on it), but stresses the need "to create an inclusive, plural and non-military-centric order beyond the US-China rival order formulations," while also restating key ASEAN principles like respect for state sovereignty, peaceful relations among regional countries and cooperation among ASEAN and its partners.[32] Straying from the ideological, exclusionary and militaristic tone of the FOIP project, ASEAN attempted to give its own imprint to this rebranding exercise, aimed at shifting the epicenter in that part of the world from China to India.

Perhaps counterintuitively, and despite the unabated US-China tensions in Asia and elsewhere, ASEAN's perspective on the Indo-Pacific did not go unnoticed either in Washington or in Beijing. From both capitals accommodative signals were emitted. The US government underlined the need to harmonize the goals of the ASEAN outlook, the FOIP and the Quad, and reiterated its commitment to ASEAN centrality.[33] China, on the other hand, despite its earlier critical stance on the very notion of the Indo-Pacific, did not object to the ASEAN outlook on it, and made its peace with it.[34] It was another case of the difference that deft diplomatic handling of sensitive security matters can make – something made possible by the type of diplomatic culture developed by ASEAN over many decades, emphasizing consensus and consultation while also aiming at what has been called "impartial enmeshment."[35] By this is meant the ability to bring outside powers, including the Great Powers, into the thicket of ASEAN's various regional frameworks, making it much more difficult for them to engage in hostile actions towards ASEAN and its member states. A key factor in this is ASEAN's tradition of objectivity and impartiality in handling relations among its members and with outside powers, offering guarantees other regional entities do not necessarily provide.

A tale of two summits

A good example of the diplomatic dividends this renders can be found in the contrast between two summits held in the US in the short span of one month in the spring of 2022.

As mentioned above, it has now become customary for the US President to address the yearly ASEAN Summit, generally held in one of the member states. In 2022, however, Washington, going out of its way to court ASEAN, offered to host a US-ASEAN summit for the first time. The initial date suggested was rejected by ASEAN, as it did not fit in with its calendar, so Washington came up with an alternative date (May 12–13). In the course of these two days, delegations from the ten ASEAN member states (including eight of the ten leaders) were wined and dined at the White House and given the royal treatment. Special meetings with Senators and Representatives were scheduled on Capitol Hill, as well as with think tanks of various kinds. The extensive joint "Vision Statement" released at the end of the meeting speaks for itself in terms of the degree to which it accommodated ASEAN centrality and its priorities:

> Emphasizing the importance of adhering to key principles, shared values and norms enshrined in the Charter of the United Nations, the ASEAN Charter, the Declaration on Zone of Peace, Freedom and Neutrality (ZOPFAN), the Treaty of Amity and Cooperation in Southeast Asia (TAC), the 1982 Convention on the Law of the Sea (UNCLOS), the Treaty on the Southeast Asia Nuclear Weapon Free Zone (SEANWFZ) and the ASEAN Outlook on the Indo-Pacific (AOIP).[36]

Fighting the COVID-19 pandemic, strengthening economic ties and connectivity, promoting maritime cooperation, enhancing people-to-people connectivity, supporting sub-regional development, leveraging technologies and promoting innovation, addressing climate change, preserving peace and building trust – these were the topics addressed in the communiqué. The meeting was widely considered to have been a success.

The contrast with the 9th Summit of the Americas (SOA) held in Los Angeles from June 6 to June 10, 2022 could not have been greater. Although the SOA had been scheduled for April 2021, shortly after the inauguration of President Biden – and thus would have been an ideal instance to introduce the President to Latin American leaders and signal the contrast in his approach to the region with President Trump (who famously skipped the 2018 Lima SOA) – the meeting was postponed for a full fourteen months. Instead of Washington, it was held in Los Angeles, as far away as possible from the US capital and its power centers. Moreover, Washington's decision not to invite Cuba, Nicaragua and Venezuela to the SOA triggered pushback across Latin America and the Caribbean. At one point, the Caribbean Community (CARICOM) (which has fifteen member countries) seriously considered not attending, and was only persuaded to do so by heavy lobbying from Secretary of State Blinken. In the end, only twenty-three out of thirty-five leaders attended, in marked contrast with the thirty-four who attended the Panama Summit in 2015. The Mexican President skipped the meeting. There was no final summit declaration, only a "Los Angeles Declaration on Migration and Protection," signed by twenty countries. The meeting was widely considered to have been a fiasco.[37]

A key factor in the failure of the SOA Summit in Los Angeles was the refusal of the US to invite Cuba, Nicaragua and Venezuela, all members of the Community of Latin American and Caribbean States (CELAC, in the Spanish-language acronym), Latin America's regional umbrella organization. The argument given by the State Department was that they were not democracies, and therefore had no place at the SOA Summit. Yet, much as Cuba, both Laos and Vietnam are one-party states, and the US had no objection to their participating in the US-ASEAN Special Summit. In fact, most observers would agree that, if Washington had *not* invited Laos and Vietnam, the latter meeting would not have taken place, as such behavior would have been considered an affront to ASEAN. But somehow Washington considered that not inviting these three Latin American countries to the SOA was perfectly acceptable behavior.

Our point is a simple one. ASEAN over time has evolved into a body known for its impartiality, sense of self ("ASEAN centrality") and non-aligned behavior – features that give guarantees to all parties with which it interacts. ASEAN is therefore respected and treated, if not as an equal, at least as a partner to be taken seriously by the Great Powers. Regional organizations in Latin America, whether CELAC, the now recovering Union of South American Nations (UNASUR), and even more limited ones, like the Southern Common Market (MERCOSUR), are still far from achieving such a status, and the results are there for all to see. Latin America is not treated the same way as ASEAN is by the Great Powers, and it shows.

Conclusion

This chapter started by asking the question whether geography is destiny, and whether smaller powers are ultimately bound to have to bandwagon, that is, to acquiesce to the whims and wishes of the Great Power with whom they share a neighborhood. To answer this question, we examined the case of ASEAN, an entity that has been around since 1967, located in the immediate neighborhood of China, in a part of the world that underwent serious conflicts in much of the twentieth century. What we found is an international organization that has succeeded in bringing together what was once a highly fragmented and divided region ("the Balkans of Asia"), and in so doing made it possible for it to grow at high rates, while also becoming a significant diplomatic interlocutor on the world stage. This has allowed ASEAN to punch above its weight, as shown by the regularity with which world leaders attend its yearly summits, and the fact that they defer to ASEAN on a variety of aspects of regional politics.

This was achieved not by simply bandwagoning to China, nor by balancing it against the United States, but by following a foreign policy of non-alignment, which draws on the region's historical association with such an approach but adapts it to the very different conditions of the new century. In many ways, ASEAN's deft diplomacy has proved to be especially adept at "playing the field" with China and with the US, making the most of its strategic geographical location to maximize the benefits it can extract from both.

Southeast Asian nations have thus elevated hedging, that is, mitigating risk under uncertain conditions, to an art form. As Kuik has observed in what he refers to as Malaysia's "paradoxical pragmatism," hedging does not mean simply taking a *middle* position between the Great Powers, but taking an *opposite* one, deploying a variety of seemingly contradictory measures (i.e., occasional defiance and occasional deference), depending on the circumstances.[38] Rather than hitching their fate to one or the other of the Great Powers, what countries in Southeast Asia do is to effectively follow a policy of non-alignment, to safeguard their own interests. Indonesia, by far the largest of ASEAN members, and the country where the seeds of the Non-Aligned Movement (NAM) were planted at the 1955 Bandung Conference, is especially explicit about its non-aligned policy,[39] something that led it as far as reconsidering its application to join the BRICS group in 2023, on the reasoning that it might compromise this commitment to non-alignment. Yet, other member states, including Singapore, in many ways a close partner of the US, also insist to both Beijing and Washington that they should *not* attempt to make Southeast Asians choose sides in the burgeoning tensions of this Second Cold War that some observers see in the making.[40] Perhaps the most remarkable and audacious of these foreign policies is the so-called "bamboo diplomacy" practiced by Vietnam, the one ASEAN member state to have fought wars with *both* the United States and with China (and defeated both of them), and that now proudly proclaims comprehensive strategic partnerships with the US *and* with China, while also keeping high levels of defense cooperation with Russia.[41]

As these various instances reflect, a signature feature of this approach to foreign policymaking is its *proactive* character. In marked contrast to the *defensive* nature of the Non-Aligned Movement in the twentieth century, the non-alignment of the new century is on the constant lookout for opportunities to enhance the margin of maneuver available to smaller states. The 2012 launching of the RCEP project, signed in 2020, and by now the largest trade agreement anywhere, is a good example of this. The same goes for ASEAN's deft handling of China's BRI and of the US's FOIP.

A key factor behind ASEAN's economic and diplomatic success has been the strength of the regional imperative, which has acted as a significant force multiplier. In that regard, the contrast with Latin America, where centripetal forces have tended to prevail over longstanding efforts to create enduring regional bodies, could not be greater. And the effects of this on their respective economic performances should not be minimized. The populations of Latin America and of ASEAN are roughly comparable, at around 650 million, and although Latin America's per capita income has traditionally been much higher than ASEAN's, this difference has been shrinking: in the year 2000 it was 3.6 times larger, but in 2022, it was less than two times larger. In other words, while ASEAN has been growing in leaps and bounds, Latin America has been stagnating and falling behind.

What is noteworthy, though, is the degree to which Latin American regionalism, despite the many occasions on which it has been given up for dead, has resurrected and returned with a vengeance. It is in such a setting that we have seen the upsurge, however imperfect, of ANA in the Americas in recent years, which is the subject of the next chapter.

6

From the Extreme West to Active Non-Alignment

In the early months of 2024, a scarce two years after coming out of the COVID-19 pandemic that affected Latin America proportionally more than any other part of the world, the region was hit by another plague, this time, dengue fever. Fomented by climate change, which in raising temperatures facilitates the breeding of the *Aedes* mosquito that spreads the disease, and helped by El Niño, the Pacific Ocean weather system, dengue is now to be found even in countries with a Mediterranean climate, like Chile and Uruguay, far removed from its traditional lands like Brazil. The Brazilian Army is once again erecting field hospitals in Brasília, and basic items like mosquito repellent spray are running out across South America. Once again, it seems that this highly urbanized region, with its myriad shantytowns and ubiquitous pools of still water, ideally suited for the quick spread of yet another plague, is succumbing to another wave of disease. Though by no means as deadly as COVID-19, dengue can kill you, and it does.[1]

Given its relative geographic isolation from the rest of the world and the specificity of its environmental conditions, one could have expected that Latin America by now would have undertaken a joint effort to address the root causes of communicable and other diseases in the lands South of the Rio Grande. A major Latin American research center on tropical and other such diseases, doing work on ways to prevent and to cure such maladies, would, after all, only be following in the footsteps of what has been done elsewhere. In 1946, the United States established what is now the premier center of this kind, the Center for Disease Control and Prevention (CDC), headquartered in Atlanta. The immediate trigger for its establishment was the need to fight malaria, especially widespread across the Southern US at the time, but it later evolved into the much more ambitious medical research organization it is today. Not to be left behind, Europe followed suit, and in 2005 established the European Center for Disease Control and Prevention, an agency of the European Union headquartered in the Swedish city of Solna, with a staff of 300. And in 2017, Africa launched the Africa Centres for Disease Control and Prevention, headquartered in Addis Ababa, Ethiopia, dependent on the African Union, and with branches across the continent.

Yet, in Latin America, no such initiative to cope with what is, after all, a major threat to the very lives of Latin Americans, and which should thus be a key governmental priority, is being considered, and is unlikely to be so soon. In fact, not only is no progress being made on the subject, but some of the progress that was made has been undone. This occurred in Chile, which for over a century had a lab associated with the University of Chile that did research and produced vaccines; after it was defunded during the military dictatorship, the country was left with no means of producing its own vaccines, something that would come to haunt it during the COVID-19 pandemic.[2] This reflects a deeper problem related to the historical trajectory of the region in the past seventy years or so.

At the end of World War II, the region emerged as a considerable force, making important contributions to the debates on the establishment of the Bretton Woods institutions and to the drafting of such significant documents as the United Nations Human Rights Charter.[3] Twenty out of the fifty-one members of the newly created UN organization in 1945 were Latin American, and the sky seemed to be the limit in terms of what could be achieved. Emblematic of this "can-do" attitude that permeated at least part of the region at the time was the presidency of Juscelino Kubitschek in Brazil (1956–61), with his "Fifty Years in Five" project to kickstart Brazilian growth and progress. It included such ambitious undertakings as moving the capital from Rio de Janeiro to Brasília, and populating the country's vast and mostly unoccupied hinterland. It also contemplated Operación Panamericana, a hemispheric undertaking to foster industrialization and modernization, designed to foster stronger links between the US and Latin America, a project for which Kubitschek enlisted such luminaries as Alberto Lleras Camargo, the President of Colombia, and Arturo Frondizi, the President of Argentina. Operación Panamericana never gained much traction with the Eisenhower administration, but it laid the foundations for the Alliance for Progress during the presidency of John F. Kennedy,[4] still today considered the most farsighted and forward-looking US policy program towards Latin America. Yet, these hopes that seemed to foreordain a future of prosperity and development for the region were dashed. Instead, the past six decades have led to something very different – a history of political instability, criminal violence, social inequality, drug trafficking and irregular migration.

The contrast with what would emerge as the European project in the 1960s, leading to what is today the European Union, on the one hand, and what would happen in Southeast Asia, with ASEAN, as discussed in the previous chapter, on the other, could not be greater. In the new century, of course, the Asia-Pacific has emerged as the world's most dynamic region in terms of growth, relative weight in international trade, and finance and innovation.[5]

A region in reverse gear

Latin America went in the opposite direction. Between 1820 and 1980, its share in the world economy increased persistently, from less than 2 percent of global GDP to around 9.5 percent (Figure 6.1). This was higher than the region's share of the world's population, at 8 percent. Yet, from the late 1970s onwards, the region's economic share began to decline to the point that, by 2019, it had fallen to a share equivalent to that of the 1950s. This was the result of the high growth of the Asia-Pacific and of the loss of dynamism in the region itself. As of 2024, the region's share of world GDP is around 7 percent, below its share of the global population – at 662 million, 8.27 percent of the total (8 billion).

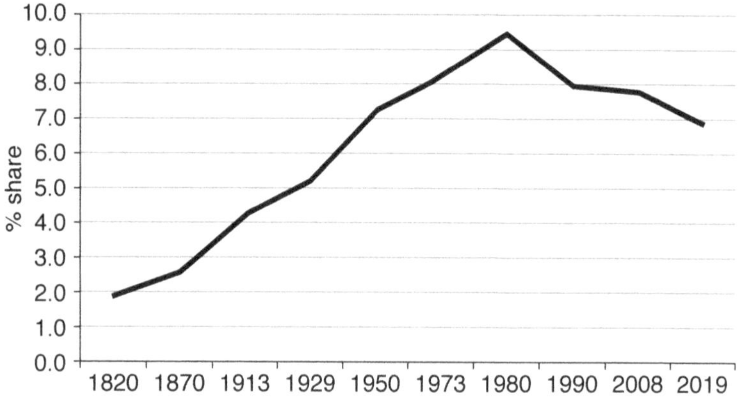

Figure 6.1 Latin America's % share of global GDP
Source: Calculated by the authors, based on ECLAC data.

According to data from the UN Economic Commission for Latin America and the Caribbean, tracking the historical trajectory of GDP per capita adjusted by purchasing power parity from 1940, GDP per capita in the region grew at a rate above that of the world average, peaking in 1980, but has steadily declined since then (Figure 6.2).

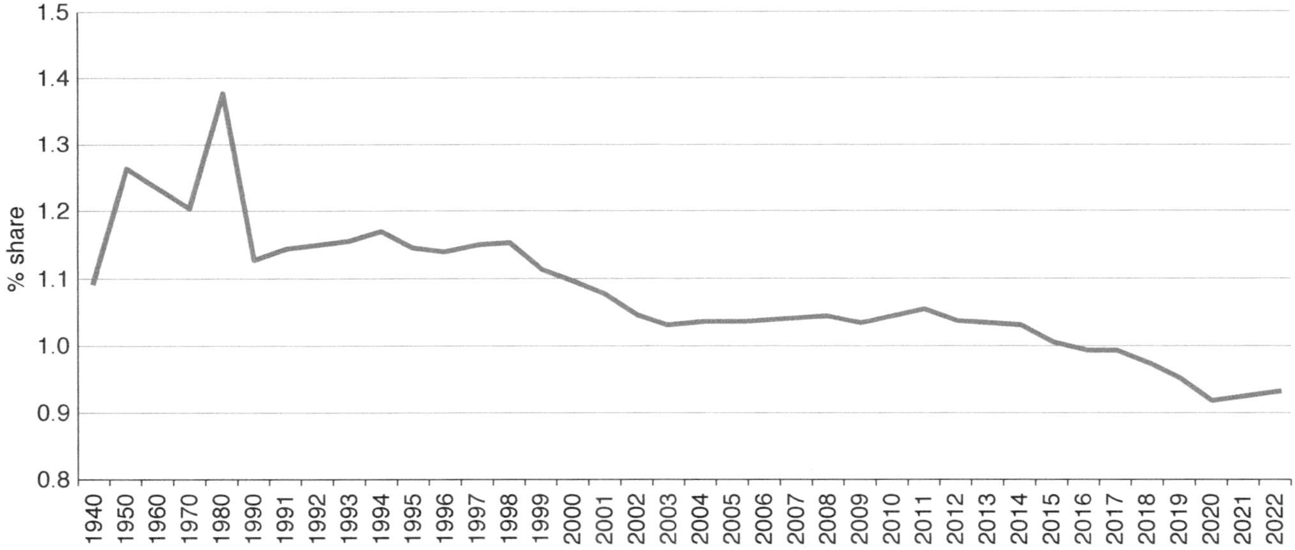

Figure 6.2 Evolution of Latin America's per capita income in relation to average global per capita income

Source: Calculated by the authors, based on ECLAC data.

As far as international trade is concerned, the picture is even bleaker. The region's exports as a share of the total fell from 12 percent in 1948 over the next four decades (as can be seen in Figure 6.3), before stabilizing from the year 2000 onwards at around 6 percent, well below the region's share of the total population. And if Mexico, whose economy is closely tied to that of the US, is excluded from these figures, the region's share of world exports drops below 3.5 percent (Figure 6.4).

These exports, in turn, are mostly composed of commodities and natural resources, without much value added. Thus, towards the end of the 1990s, and until 2010, exports of primary products (including precious stones and non-monetary gold) represented between 10 and 12 percent of the world's total. From 2010 this started to decline, and it currently stands below 9 percent, as can be seen from Figure 6.5. Venezuela, Brazil, Colombia and Ecuador are significant oil producers. In contrast, as can be seen from Figure 6.6, the region's share in exports of manufactured goods has never exceeded 5 percent of the world total and is currently below 4 percent of the latter.

As far as technology is concerned, the region's role is marginal. In fact, there are no major technological innovations that have been generated there. On the assumption that one need not invest in research and development (R&D), but simply buy foreign technologies, Latin America is, with a few exceptions, a passive recipient of such technologies, lacking even the capacity to unpack them to further adapt them to the region's specific needs. In fact, save for Brazil, no country in the region invests more than 1 percent of GDP in R&D, and total spending on R&D in Latin America is lower than that of three leading US universities, Johns Hopkins, MIT and Stanford.

In such a context, it should not be surprising that, faced with major challenges, the region is unable to respond adequately. As has been pointed out, "By the end of 2021, ten of the forty countries across the globe with the most COVID-19 deaths per capita were in Latin America," with Peru at the very top and

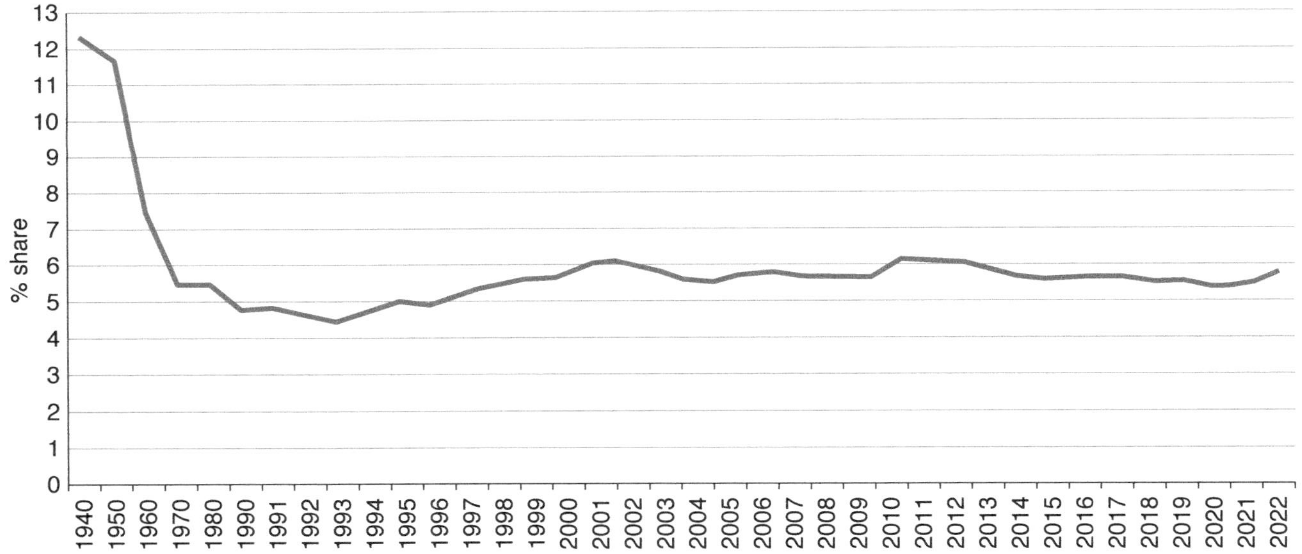

Figure 6.3 Exports from Latin America and the Caribbean (as % share of global exports)

Source: Calculated by the authors, based on ECLAC data.

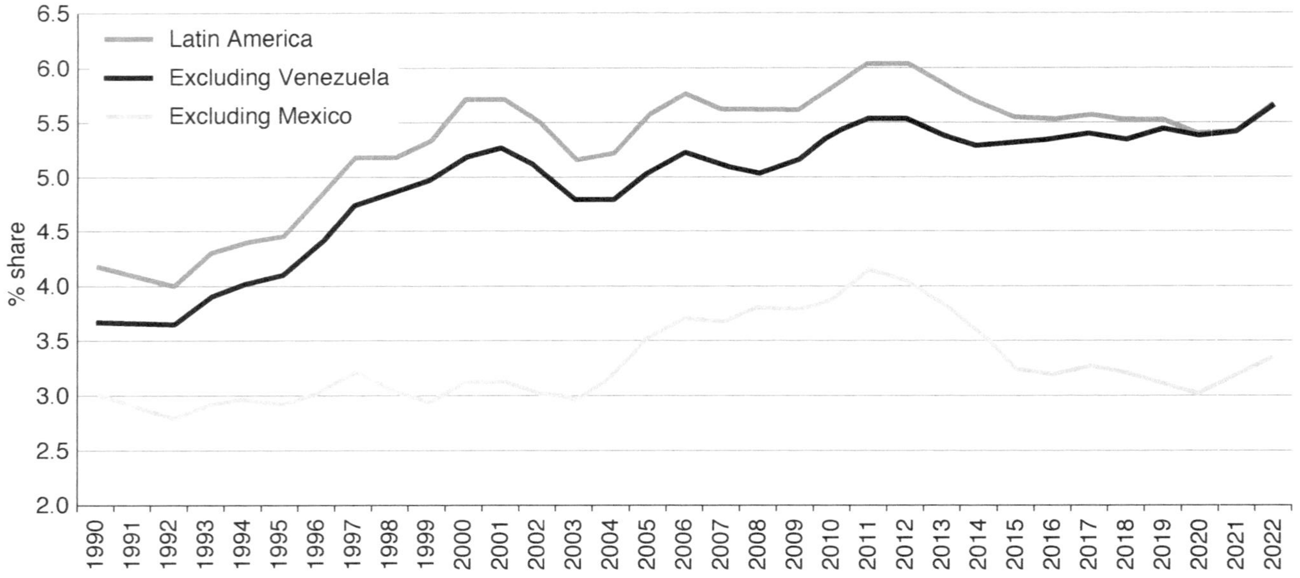

Figure 6.4 Latin America's % share of world exports

Source: Calculated by the authors, based on ECLAC data.

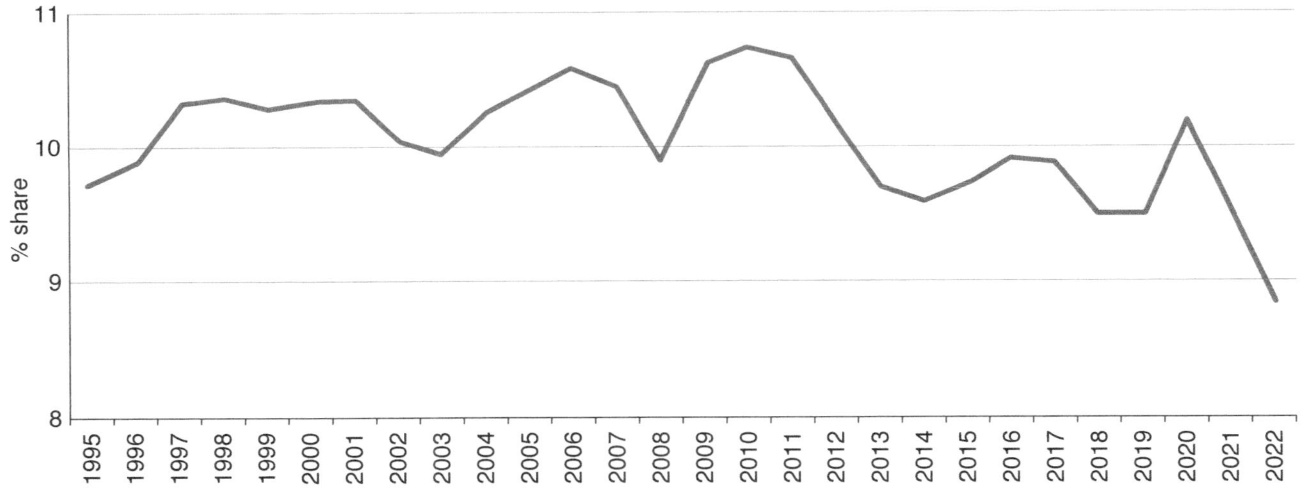

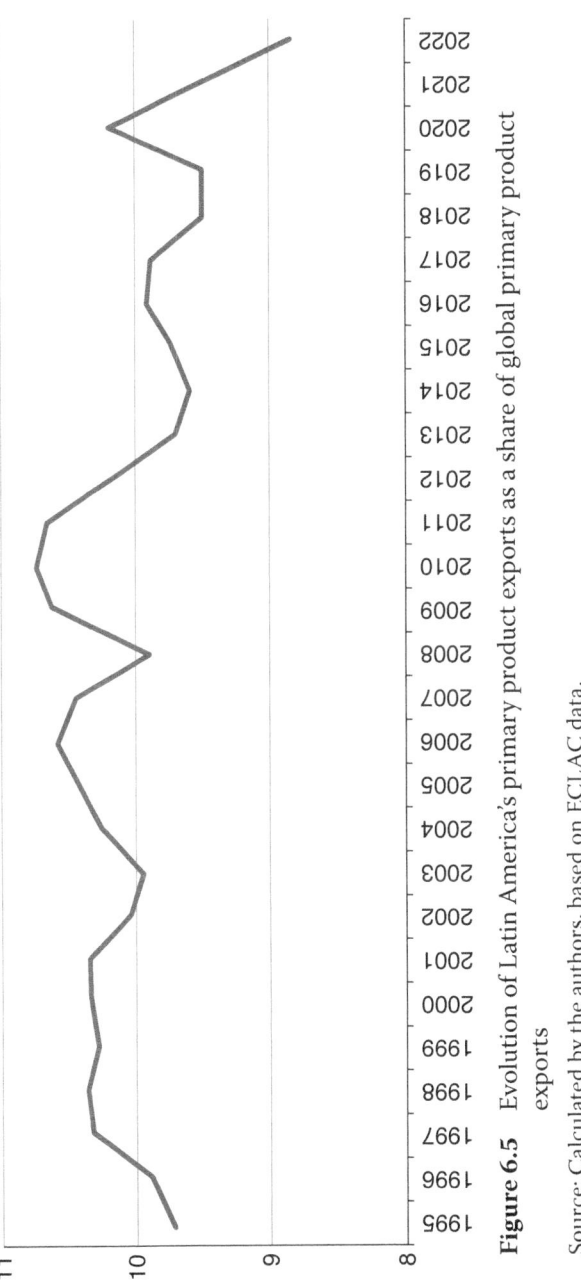

Figure 6.5 Evolution of Latin America's primary product exports as a share of global primary product exports

Source: Calculated by the authors, based on ECLAC data.

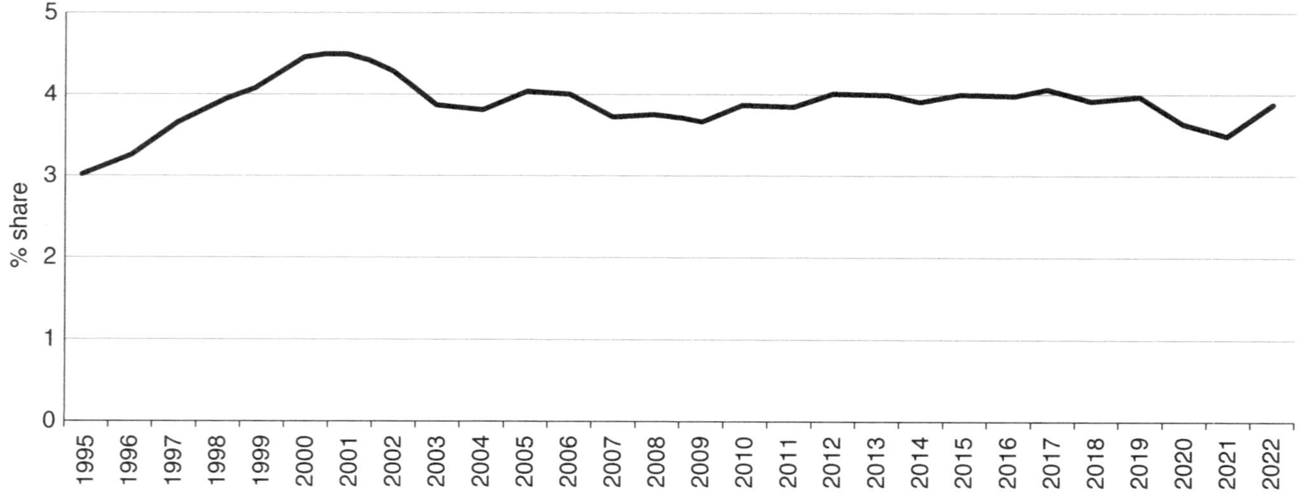

Figure 6.6 Exports of manufactured products by Latin America (as % share of global total)

Source: Calculated by the authors, based on ECLAC data.

Brazil and Argentina among the top twenty.[6] And although regional GDP managed to recover in 2021 to 6.1 percent growth (after plummeting in 2020 by −6.6 percent, the steepest fall of any region), soon it was back to business as usual, with 2.3 percent growth in 2023 and a projected growth of 2.0 percent in 2024, again, the lowest of any region in the world, with the exception of Europe.[7]

This economic stagnation goes hand in hand with a declining international influence. The last significant global initiative of Latin American origin was the World Summit on Social Development held in Copenhagen in 1995, arising out of a Chilean proposal. At the meeting, governments committed to eradicating poverty, promoting productive employment and fostering social integration. Together with the action program that was approved there, the summit constitutes the direct antecedent of the UN 2030 Agenda with its seventeen global objectives for a better and sustainable future for all, established in 2015 by the UN General Assembly. A new Social Summit will be held in 2025 in New York.

In recent years, the decline of Latin America's presence in international organizations is also notable. Traditionally, there had been quite a few Latin Americans at the helm of UN agencies, such as UNCTAD, the WTO, the World Food Organization, UN Women, the International Labor Organization (ILO) and the United Nations High Commission for Human Rights (UNHCR), among other entities. In 2024, only two of the smaller seventeen UN agencies, the International Atomic Energy Organization (IAEA) and the World Meteorological Organization (WMO), are headed by Latin Americans. All of this points to the fact that, if the region wants to stop this seeming slide into international marginality, if not downright irrelevancy, it must change its approach to foreign policy and the way it interacts with the rest of the world. This is the subject to which we now turn, where developments in the Peruvian port of Chancay illustrate the enormous opportunities such a new approach entails, but also the considerable demands it generates for its successful application.

Chancay, China and ANA

In what is the biggest infrastructure project in South America today, some 70 km North of Lima, a gigantic, $3.6 billion, deep-water port is being built in what used to be a sleepy fishing village by the name of Chancay. Peru, one of the fastest growing South American countries for much of the new century, and one of only six countries in the world to have free trade agreements both with the United States and with China, targeted Asia as a growth market as far back as the 1990s. It has done very well as a result. One effect of its huge trade with Asia (China is Peru's number-one trading partner) has been that Peru's main port, Callao, is overwhelmed and unable to handle more cargo. The new port is being built in partnership with the Chinese company COSCO Shipping Ports, one of the giants in the field. Five years in the making, it was inaugurated in November 2024 by none other than President Xi Jinping himself, who attended the APEC Leaders' Meeting held in Lima that month[8]

And Peru is by no means limiting its high expectations for Chancay to its own trans-Pacific trade. It sees the mega-port as a gateway from South America to Asia, capable of receiving the biggest cargo ships, with up to 18,000 containers, and starting its operations with four docks that may be expanded up to fifteen. The plan is to make Chancay a hub for exports to Asia from neighboring countries as well, with Brazil having already expressed its interest in relying on it for its massive soybean exports to China. Chile, on the other hand, which has traditionally seen itself as South America's gateway to Asia, is lagging badly behind in its own mega-port project in its central littoral, which has been on the table for more than a decade now, but is unlikely to see the light of day before 2040. Not unreasonably, the Peruvian government says that Chancay will give Peru a leg up in its competition with Chile in the Asia-Pacific.

In a region with a huge infrastructure deficit, which badly affects its productivity and international competitiveness, one would expect such a project to be universally welcome. Yet, that has not been the case.

According to the *Financial Times*: "The US has expressed concern to Peru that China is gaining control over critical parts of the South American nation's infrastructure, including electricity supply to the capital Lima and a new mega-port on the Pacific coast. . . . On the big geostrategic issues, the Peruvian government is not sufficiently focused on analysing the benefits and threats to the country," an anonymous US government official told the *FT*.[9]

In short, instead of welcoming the progress being made by Peru with one of its biggest public works ever, and one critical for its trans-Pacific trade, the US objects to it, arguing that the port might eventually be turned into a dual-use facility by the Chinese PLA Navy, and thus become a threat to the US. Should Latin American countries stop building deep-water ports and thus limit their international competitiveness to assuage such fears in Washington? Should they limit their trade with the world's fastest growing region, that is, East Asia, to satisfy US geopolitical concerns? To ask the question is to answer it, yet such are the very real dilemmas faced by weaker states as they navigate the perilous waters of Great Power competition.

China's attempts at soft balancing the US in the Western Hemisphere by emphasizing development issues like increased trade, investment, connectivity and infrastructure is what would be expected from a rising power. While the US response to it, stressing its own geopolitical concerns, while understandable, does not only not resonate, but triggers pushback. The least of Latin America's concerns are the games played by Washington and Beijing as to who will gain primacy over the other. The region needs growth, material progress and job creation. Those powers that can provide them will have the attention of governments in the region.

Yet, there was another twist to the Chancay plot. As it turns out, when in 2019 COSCO signed the contract to build the port, with a 60 percent majority stake in it, the fine print stated that the port would be for COSCO's exclusive use. This was something the Peruvian Port Authority (APN) was apparently unaware of, until they were informed of it by the company in 2024. This put the APN in a bind, since it did not have the authority to cede such exclusive rights.[10] As Stephen Kaplan has pointed out, one difference between Western policy conditionality and Chinese commercial conditionality lies precisely in the fact that in the latter the small print is often decisive, which is what was overlooked by the Peruvian authorities in the case of Chancay.[11]

Our point is that it is these differences in the approaches of the Great Powers to their relations with developing nations that can and should be leveraged by the latter, thus reducing this policy conditionality as much as possible to their advantage. And this is what Active Non-Alignment (ANA) is all about.

Active Non-Alignment as a response to Great Power competition

The concept of "Active Non-Alignment" emerged in 2019 as a conceptual tool and foreign policy recommendation for Latin American states to deal with the challenges posed by the US-China competition for hegemony,[12] and was then further developed.[13] The clearest expression of the risks and the uncertainty created by this competition was the campaign of the first Trump administration to pressure Latin American governments to reduce or even cut their economic links with China. The term "active" refers to a foreign policy that is in constant search of new opportunities, evaluating each of them on their own terms. It recognizes the historical roots of non-alignment, but adapts the concept to the realities of the new century. It requires an especially deft and skillful diplomacy, one attuned to the emerging challenges in the international environment. ANA calls on Latin American governments to not accept *a priori* and *in toto* the positions of any of the Great Powers in competition, but to define their international behavior according to their own sovereign interests without giving in to diplomatic, political or economic pressures from the hegemonic powers.

From the beginning, the concept has referred to a broader spatial and temporal scope, namely the Global South as a whole, and can be applied to situations of hegemonic conflict in general, something that became especially apparent in 2022–4. Nonetheless, ANA does not mean neutrality. The latter implies not taking positions in international issues. Switzerland, which has not joined the EU, and was not even a member of the UN until 2002, is a prime example of a policy of neutrality. ANA, on the other hand, is not about refusing to take a stand on international issues, but about refusing to align automatically with one or another of the Great Powers.[14]

The qualifier "active" also indicates that this non-alignment is perfectly compatible with taking a position (whether critical or supportive) on decisions made by the Great Powers. Each of these decisions will be evaluated on its merits without *a priori* prejudices of any kind. Neutrality implies refraining from issuing an opinion. ANA, on the contrary, signifies taking a position based on convictions. Thus, for example, in the case of the dilemma that Chile and Mexico confronted as non-permanent members of the UN Security Council in 2003, in the face of pressure from the United States to support it in a resolution endorsing the invasion of Iraq, the doctrine of neutrality would have led to them *not* making a statement one way or the other. However, *opposing* that resolution was consistent with an ANA position.[15] In turn, nothing prevents a country that embraces this doctrine from condemning, for example, practices of the Chinese government that violate human rights.

In the days of the NAM, non-alignment meant not joining the military alliances of either of the two superpowers, the United States or the Soviet Union. In the new century, in a globalized and interdependent world, this has changed. When we originally put forward the ANA proposal, some objected to it, dismissing it as nostalgic reminiscence of the past. Five years later, the term has become common currency.[16]

ANA in Latin America

Far from being a somewhat abstract, future-oriented foreign policy proposal, ANA has, in its own way, already been incorporated into the conduct of Latin American foreign relations. We have already mentioned that the issue of unilateral Western sanctions against Russia is one that has generated pushback across the Global South. It was seen as an unwarranted and unprecedented weaponization of the regular instruments of international exchange, with severely disruptive effects on the global economy.[17] In the case of Brazil, a leading agricultural producer and exporter that imports one fourth of its fertilizers from Russia, joining the sanctions would have meant sacrificing a significant share of its agricultural production.[18] Beyond Brazil's reaction to the war in Ukraine, there were precedents for a more independent behavior on the part of Brasília. Although President Bolsonaro (2019–23) headed perhaps the most pro-US Brazilian government ever, he refused to exclude Huawei from the bid for 5G networks in Brazil, despite pressure from Washington.[19]

In other words, in the past few years, most Latin American countries have already been applying a policy of non-alignment, realizing that they have very little to gain by automatically aligning with Washington or with Beijing. In this sense, ANA already constitutes an observable empirical trend, even pattern, of extant Latin American foreign policy.

This is because for Latin American countries the management of US-China tensions in the Western Hemisphere has become perhaps the most significant issue on their foreign relations agenda. On matters such as infrastructure projects, digital connectivity and the deployment of 5G technology, Washington has pressured Latin American countries not to reach agreements with Beijing. Nonetheless, even amid the pandemic and a deep economic recession, several governments in the region – left, right and center – chose to focus on their own national interests and not to automatically side with either Washington or Beijing. In addition to Brazil, what happened with Huawei was repeated in several countries across the region. As discussed in Chapter 2, Ecuador and Uruguay have stressed that it is key for the countries of the region to have options. Both countries, governed by conservative coalitions, have been keen to sign free trade agreements with China, after having been rebuffed by Washington in their attempts to sign FTAs with the United States. Obviously, a position of alignment with the US would make any such negotiations with China impossible.

The Latin American position was also made clear in 2021 at the China-CELAC Ministerial Forum (Mexico City, 2–3 December) and at the Summit for Democracy (Washington, 9–10 December). Most Latin American countries participated in both meetings and saw no contradiction in doing so.

Latin America faces an enormous challenge and, at the same time, a remarkable opportunity. The challenge lies in reintegrating after decades of regional disintegration, the opportunity in leveraging such regional unity in relation to the

Great Powers. However, this requires a fundamental political condition: Latin American convergence. ANA provides a useful guide to action in this regard.

Non-alignment across the Global South

Reactions across the Global South to the war in Ukraine, and even more so to the war in Gaza, demonstrate that ANA is not limited to Latin America but has wider global attraction and applicability. The pattern is also observable in Africa and Asia, where the NAM originated. And, as James Traub has observed, "the Western demand to close ranks behind Ukraine did not provoke a backlash so much as crystallize ways of thinking that preceded the war."[20]

Both wars have generated some common responses across the Global South, reproducing the dynamic of "the West versus the Rest." India plays a central role in the Global South's reluctance to align itself in the Russia/Ukraine conflict, despite the rapprochement in recent years between India and the US. It can be said that in this situation New Delhi has rediscovered its non-aligned roots (although it calls it multi-alignment). In Europe's greatest crisis since World War II, India is acting accordingly. As Indian political scientist Pratap Bhanu Mehta puts it: "Paradoxically, the war in Ukraine has diminished trust in Western powers and concentrated people's minds on how to hedge bets."[21]

Furthermore, seventeen African countries, including South Africa, abstained in the UN General Assembly vote on the resolution condemning the Russian invasion of Ukraine; eight countries did not vote, and one voted against it. On the UN resolution to suspend Russia from the UNHRC, nine African countries voted against it, twenty-three abstained and nine did not vote. Many others who voted in favor have nevertheless opposed the imposition of sanctions on Moscow. As discussed in the previous chapter, something similar can be said about the reaction in Southeast Asia among the ASEAN member states.

Faced with the reappearance of a confrontation between the Great Powers, an emerging Global South is picking up the traditions of the post-World War II, post-colonial movement and adapting it to the challenges of the new century.

A roadmap to step back from the brink

The impacts of the COVID-19 pandemic and the wars in Ukraine and Gaza mark a turning point in world affairs – an epochal change. To cope with the dizzying pace of change in this new scenario, new approaches are needed; the tried and true "politics as usual" of the past will not do. Enter ANA.

For Latin America, ANA provides a useful roadmap for avoiding its slippage towards irrelevancy and marginality in world affairs, and opens the possibility of defining a common position in the region. In the first Cold War, Latin American countries largely sided with the US. Why is it different this time? The answer is simple. Whereas the USSR did not have much to offer in terms of trade and investment opportunities, let alone financial cooperation, that is not the case with China, by now South America's largest trading partner. At the same time, the US, for reasons related to its domestic politics, is highly constrained in terms of the financial resources it can deploy in the region and more broadly. The same goes for granting access to the US market, limited by the increasingly anti-free trade sentiment in US public opinion. And whereas in the past there were veto players in Latin American countries (business and the military) that were able to block closer ties with the Soviet Union, it is not necessarily in their interests to do so today. Strictly from the perspective of a rational actor, therefore, the best foreign policy strategy for Latin American governments of any political hue is to keep their options open and deal with Washington and Beijing on an issue-by-issue basis, without committing *a priori* to either side.[22]

As Catherine Osborn has written, Latin America's new non-alignment may well take on a green hue, reflecting the pressing environmental priorities of a region especially vulnerable to climate change.[23] Among the new (and not so new) crop of emerging Latin American leaders, such as Gustavo Petro in Colombia, Gabriel Boric in Chile and, critically, Luiz Inacío Lula da Silva in Brazil, the issue of global warming and how to lower carbon emissions is front and center – though differences between North and South as to who should pay, and how, for such programs remain unresolved. As President Lula put it in his 2023 opening speech to the United Nations General Assembly, "the richest 10 percent of the world's population are responsible for almost half of all carbon released into the atmosphere," but "it is the vulnerable populations in the Global South who are most affected by the loss and damage caused by climate change."[24] Environmental issues may also be an anchor for building new coalitions across the Global South, and Brazil, with its strong record in entities such as the India-Brazil-South Africa initiative (IBSA) and the BRICS group, may be called upon to play a leading role.

As indicated above, ANA also has broader attraction and applicability across the Global South. By playing the field, hedging their bets and shopping for the best alternative offered in the Great Power marketplace, the countries of the Global South can make the most of this competition. Kenya under the government of President William Ruto is Exhibit A of the benefits such an approach can generate. For some time now, Kenya has been working closely with China to build up its infrastructure, as it aims to position itself as a key transport and logistics hub in East Africa. A Chinese-built railway line from Nairobi to the port of Mombasa – the first new railway line built in East Africa in a century, part of China's Belt and

Road Initiative, and a line Ruto is keen to expand further – is a concrete result of such efforts. Does this mean Kenya is totally wedded to China? By no means. While courting Beijing in this effort to strengthen its transport facilities, Kenya has not been averse to collaborating with Washington. It is doing so with something as controversial and out-of-the-box as committing to sending a 1,000-strong police force to Haiti to pacify the Caribbean island of the Black Jacobins. In this, Kenya is responding to the Biden administration's wish to outsource the policing of the by now gang-controlled failed state. *Stricto sensu*, this is something that should be done by the countries of the Western Hemisphere, and there is something slightly surreal in recruiting an East African police force to bring peace to a Caribbean island. That said, there is little doubt that the move has put Kenya in a highly advantageous position – responding to the United States in a moment of need and doing so with something as eloquent as the deployment of a significant police force halfway across the world.[25]

Finally, is there a specific case in Latin America that sheds light on what implementing ANA is all about? As it happens, there is.

ANA in practice: Brazil in Lula's third term

In many ways, ANA is exactly what has taken place in the first eighteenth months of President Lula's third term (2023–7) in Brazil. The largest country in the region, and one with a strong diplomatic tradition, Brazil is known for its independent foreign policy and its unwillingness to subordinate its priorities to those of the Great Powers.[26] In the recent past, this has expressed itself in a highly assertive foreign policy under the presidencies of Fernando Henrique Cardoso (1995–2003) and Lula da Silva (2003–11), albeit one that was interrupted under the government of Jair Bolsonaro (2019–23). However, with the return of Lula to Planalto, Brasília's presidential palace, the country resumed what Celso Amorim has referred to as its "política exterior activa y altiva."[27]

Despite Brazil's many domestic challenges, shortly after his inauguration, President Lula started to promote a peace plan for Ukraine and to display an ambitious strategy to support it. This led to a visit to Washington in February 2023 in which he proposed to President Biden the creation of a "peace club" made up of a group of countries that would facilitate a dialogue between Russia and Ukraine. The group would include rising powers like China, India, Indonesia and Turkey. In March 2023, Lula had an extensive teleconference with President Zelensky of Ukraine; this was followed by a visit to Moscow by Celso Amorim, his chief foreign affairs advisor, where, breaking protocol, Amorim was received by President Putin himself. In turn, Lula continued to promote his peace plan, this time with President Xi Jinping, in a visit he made to Beijing in April 2023. All of this has been made possible because Brazil has kept a non-aligned position on the war in Ukraine, refusing to support either side. Instead of ignoring the conflict, however, Brazil has displayed a dynamic, proactive diplomacy, committed to bringing about peace and ending the war, a position very different from that of Western powers who have signaled their preference for it to go on "for as long as it takes."[28]

At the same time, understanding that ANA requires a strong dose of regional cooperation, Brazil has provided a new impetus to cooperation in Latin America. In January 2023, Lula played a leading role in the CELAC Summit held in Buenos Aires under the Argentina presidency, where Brazil's return was hailed like that of the prodigal son (one of the first measures of the Bolsonaro administration in 2019 had been to announce that Brazil would leave CELAC). In May 2023, Lula called a South American summit that was held in Brasília, the first in eight years. And in August he held an Amazonian summit in Belém of Pará, with the participation of eight South

American heads of state that share the Amazonian Basin, to discuss how to best preserve the Amazonian forest and thus diminish the dangers of climate change that threaten planet Earth.

On the global stage, in October 2023, as chair of the UN Security Council, Brazil submitted a resolution calling for a ceasefire in Gaza; that resolution was ultimately vetoed by the US, but Brazil has continued to press for an end to the war in Gaza in a variety of ways. In 2024, as chair of the G20 – and continuing along the lines of its two predecessors in that position, Indonesia in 2022 and India in 2023 – Brazil pushed for developmental (as opposed to strictly geopolitical) concerns to be put front and center of the global governance agenda. Brazil is also gearing up to chair COP30 in 2025, in what is expected to be a significant opportunity for it to make progress in the worldwide effort to reduce carbon emissions, as well as the BRICS+ group.[29]

This is an agenda that is still very much being unrolled, and it has not been without setbacks. But its sheer scope and range shows what ANA is all about.

Conclusion

Latin America was late to join the Non-Aligned Movement. No Latin American head of government was present at the Bandung Conference in 1955. The only one present at the founding of the NAM itself, in Belgrade in 1961, was Cuba's Fidel Castro – though subsequently many countries from the region were to become part of the Movement. In the case of Active Non-Alignment, however, it has been Latin America that has taken the lead in crafting and applying a foreign policy doctrine that came into its own as the region found itself between a rock and a hard place, with both Washington and Beijing vying for predominance across the Americas.

At first, this seems unlikely. For much of its independent history, the unquestioned hegemon in the Western Hemisphere has been the United States. China was not just geographically, but also politically, economically and culturally far removed from the lands South of the Rio Grande. Yet, in what is perhaps the most significant change in Latin America's international political economy in two centuries, in the first quarter of the new century China has emerged as a key economic partner for Latin America. In South America this is so much the case that China is by now the number one trading partner in the region, displacing both the US and Europe. This creates its own foreign policy imperatives. A state visit to Beijing with a huge business delegation has now become almost a rite of passage for Latin American presidents – eight of them did so in 2023. In turn, President Xi Jinping visited more Latin American countries in 2013–19 (eleven) than presidents Trump and Biden *combined* did in 2017–24 (three).

Yet, the issue goes beyond trade and investment flows (Chinese investment in Latin America, though lagging behind trade, is also a force to reckon with) and presidential visits and speaks to the extant dynamic at play in the relationship between a declining hegemon and a rising power. Hegemons are expected to provide a variety of global public goods, something that legitimizes and strengthens their predominance at the helm of the international system. However, once hegemonic decline sets in, at some point a domestic revolt against that very system takes place, on the strength of the argument that "the world is taking advantage of us." At that point, Great Powers turn inward – thus, the denunciation of "globalism," and the rise of protectionism and isolationism – and start to cut back on their contributions to international development. Rising powers, on the other hand, feel no such compulsions. On the contrary, they see this an opportunity, and step up their game, particularly on the economic and development front, in their attempt to win the hearts and minds of weaker states, for whose favor they compete with the hegemon. They do so while carefully steering clear of the defense and military sectors, which are much more sensitive and bound to raise alarms in the hegemon's capital.

In many ways, this is exactly what is happening in the triangular relationship between the US, China and Latin America. For developing Latin American states, this presents a special challenge. On the one hand, the longstanding relationship with the US needs to be kept on an even keel. The US is still the largest economy in the world, and its most significant scientific and technological power, as well as the main trading partner for countries in the Northern part of Latin America, the states around the Caribbean Basin. On the other hand, and this is particularly true for South American nations, some of the most dynamic trade and investment opportunities are now coming out of China. This is something that incumbent governments, in a region regularly affected by economic crises of various kinds, ignore at their peril. To manage this delicate balancing act, ANA offers the best kit of tools.

If this is true for Latin America, is it also the case for Africa and Asia? This is the subject of the next chapter, in which we explore the rise of the Global South and the degree to which ANA goes hand in hand with it.

7

The Global South and Active Non-Alignment

Most international summits tend to be subdued, behind-closed-doors affairs, far removed from the citizenry of the host country. Not the 18th G20 Summit held in New Delhi in September 2023. As any visitor to the Indian capital at the time could attest, from the moment one entered Indira Gandhi International Airport, one could not miss the banners about the meeting, banners that were also plastered around much of the city. Over the preceding year, hundreds of meetings were held across the country to discuss the G20 agenda and the contribution India could make to it while also furthering its own development goals. It is estimated that some 100,000 foreign delegates visited India in the year running up to the summit, and that 15 million Indians participated in G20-related events. Cultural events on the G20 theme were held in all Indian states. Never in the history of G20 summits had the host government reached so deeply into civil society to make this gathering of world leaders relevant to its citizens.

The G20 brings together developed nations, rising powers and developing countries to deal with the challenges posed by global economic governance.[1] The Indian presidency in 2022–3 aimed to enhance the country's standing as an aspiring leader of the Global South by holding a variety of preceding conferences designed to capture "the voice of the Global South." In the previous two decades, India had cut an increasingly large shadow in world affairs through entities like IBSA, the BRICS, the Shanghai Cooperation Organization (SCO), as well as the G20 itself, and this summit was the culmination, the crowning glory, of all these previous efforts, a coronation of sorts for India's strongest leader since Indira Gandhi, Narendra Modi, ahead of his gearing up for reelection in 2024.[2]

Yet, there was concern in New Delhi's corridors of power. The success of diplomatic summits is measured by two indicators: the number and relative significance of the attending leaders and the final declaration. On both counts, there were good reasons to be worried. It had been known for some time that President Vladimir Putin of Russia would not attend, given the warrant for his arrest issued by the International Criminal Court for war crimes allegedly committed by Russia in the war in Ukraine. There was also uncertainty about the attendance of President Xi Jinping of China – who eventually notified only a few days before the meeting that he would not be present. And the fact that Dr. Jill Biden, the US First Lady, was affected by COVID-19 in the week before the meeting raised doubts about whether the US President himself would travel to New Delhi. In turn, given the very different perspectives of the member countries on the war in Ukraine, there was skepticism as to whether any sort of final declaration could be agreed on. So much so that in the days before the summit, UN Secretary-General António Guterres had gone so far as to label the world "a dysfunctional family."[3]

Yet, despite the pre-summit premonitions and the warnings of naysayers, things turned out well. President Biden did attend and played a constructive role, yet was careful not to steal the limelight from Prime Minister Modi, whose show it was. There was an extended and ambitious thirty-eight-paragraph final declaration, which cleverly side-stepped the issue of the

Ukraine war. It stressed the urgency of dealing with the challenges of climate change and of improving the operation of multilateral development banks, among other subjects. The African Union was incorporated as a full member, much as the European Union has been from the beginning.[4]

The 18th G20 Summit was thus considered an unmitigated success and quite a feather in India's diplomatic cap. In the context of a highly divisive war and many international tensions, India was able to host and bring to a fruitful conclusion a meeting of world leaders from several countries, developed and developing, capitalist and socialist, large and small. Beyond that, for the reasons mentioned above, and given the historical role that India has played in the post-colonial world, the summit could also be considered as the coming of age of the Global South in the new century, much as the 2008 Olympic Games were seen as the coming of age of contemporary China. With G20 summits held in Indonesia in 2022 and in Brazil in 2024, rising powers from the Global South have been able to set an agenda stressing the priorities of developing nations, like debt financing, food security and climate change. This was reinforced by the fact that the New Delhi meeting was preceded by the 15th BRICS Summit in Johannesburg in August 2023, which led to the group's expansion, about which more below. All this contrasts with the G7, which has focused on geopolitics and the war in Ukraine.

In previous chapters, we have discussed how Active Non-Alignment came about in 2019–20 as a doctrine to enable Latin America to deal with the rift created by US-China tensions and the ensuing fault-line in the international system, with both Washington and Beijing vying for hegemony. Though generated in and for Latin America, ANA as a foreign policy approach was formulated in such a way that it was also applicable elsewhere. Since then, as we have seen, the wars in Ukraine and Gaza have brought to the fore another, hitherto less visible fault-line in world politics, that between the developed countries of the West and the other, less developed nations. The point has been made by former French Prime Minister Dominique de Villepin, who, speaking in October 2023 about the conflict in Gaza, referred to "an international context of profound division of the world, a very important fracture of the world which we have also seen in Ukraine with, on the one side, the West, and on the other, what we call the Global South, that is, the rest of the world."[5]

There is no doubt that these wars have highlighted extant differences between North and South that were less apparent before. That said, it is also evident that the causes of this division are of a deeper nature.

The rise of the Global South

Although the term "Global South" has been around for more than half a century and has become the term of choice to refer to the developing world, it is not uncontested. It was first used in 1969 by American activist Carl Oglesby in discussing the Vietnam War, which he argued was the result of the "North's dominance over the global south."[6] Yet, at the time, the more common denomination for the countries of Africa, Asia and Latin America was "the Third World," originally coined by French demographer Alfred Sauvy in 1952, drawing on the French three estates (clergy, nobility and commoners). In this categorization, the developed capitalist nations constituted the First World, the socialist ones in the Soviet orbit the Second World and the developing nations the Third World. Although the Non-Aligned Movement's attempts to press for a New International Economic Order in the 1970s and 1980s (and the ensuing Brandt Report on the subject) gave some currency to the term, it was not until the 1990s, after the fall of the Berlin Wall and the end of the Soviet Union, that "Global South" started to be more widely used.[7]

A common criticism of the term is that it is too vague and imprecise to be useful.[8] Yet, as we noted in Chapter 1, it is not a geographical term, but a geopolitical one. The two largest members, China and India, are in the Northern Hemisphere, as are others. In contrast to countries in the developed North – i.e., North America, Europe, plus Japan and Australasia – those in the Global South tend to be poorer, with a colonial past and often an economic dependence on developed nations. A 2004 United Nations Development Program (UNDP) report provides a list of 143 countries belonging to the Global South; their regional distribution is shown in Table 7.1.[9]

Table 7.1 The Global South (number of countries)

Africa	47
North Africa	6
Asia	23
Central Asia	8
West Asia	14
Pacific Islands	12
Latin America	19
Caribbean	13
Total	**142**

Source: Authors' table based on data from the United Nations Development Program, Forging a Global South: United Nations Day for South-South Cooperation, December 19, 2004, https://www.undp.org/sites/g/files/zskgke326/files/migration/cn/UNDP-CH-PR-Publications-UNDay-for-South-South-Cooperation.pdf.

The list in effect includes all countries that are not members of the OECD or the EU, except for Chile, Colombia, Costa Rica, Cyprus, Mexico, South Korea and Turkey, and excluding also the Balkan states of Albania, Bosnia and Herzegovina, Kosovo, Montenegro, North Macedonia and Serbia, as well as Russia and Belarus. In this tally, the Global North is composed of thirty-six countries. The list is longer than the membership of the two groups that purport to represent developing nations, namely the NAM (120 members, with fourteen observers, including four that are not in the Global South list) and the G77 (134 members).

Not surprisingly, as the Global South has raised its profile in world politics, the very use of the term has elicited pushback, with several commentators calling for it to be retired on the grounds of it being imprecise – a "catch-all" term encompassing a group so heterogeneous that it would be unable to undertake any concerted action. Perhaps the most remarkable objection to it is that it is divisive, "a catalyst for political polarization," and thus presumably dangerous.[10] The notion that the terms we use in sociopolitical analysis should only contribute to consensus-building is quite novel as well as beside the point. It is also ironic that the very same people praising the newfound unity of the West in the wake of the Russian invasion of Ukraine should find any concerted action on the part of the Global South a dangerous proposition.

Yes, there are significant differences among the many countries that comprise the Global South. Yet, as Sarang Shidore has argued, they have one thing in common: the sense that they have been largely excluded from global governance and would now like to have a place at the table of high international politics.[11] They also believe that current international arrangements do not respond to their needs and priorities. They are thus *demandeurs* of change on a variety of fronts. With the international order now prioritizing conflict over cooperation, they consider that Great Power competition focused on one-upmanship rather than on solving global problems is especially harmful to their concerns. As Cuban President Miguel Díaz-Canel put it at the opening of the G77+China summit in Havana in September 2023: "After all this time that the North has organized the world according to its interests, it is now up to the South to change the rules of the game."[12] As a product of this – in what seemed to some like a throwback to earlier times, but reflecting very much the mood of countries that feel excluded from an international system they consider to be both inequitable and unjust – in December 2022 the United Nations General Assembly passed a resolution entitled "Towards a New International Economic Order," bringing back to the fore the NIEO, which had been the main battle horse of the Non-Aligned Movement in the 1970s and 1980s. Not surprisingly, the vote split along the North-South cleavage line we have been discussing in this book.[13]

What does the Global South want?

Beyond the differences among the countries that make up the Global South, there is also a convergence of views along five central axes:

(1) Geopolitical: the affirmation of the autonomy of states to adopt international policies and positions based on their national interests, independently of the policies and positions of the Great Powers.
(2) Multilateral: discontent with current arrangements at major international organizations, which do not reflect the realities of the new century.
(3) Political/economic: dissatisfaction with the degree to which the structure and functioning of the global economy are dominated by developed country actors – governmental, intergovernmental and private.
(4) The economic sanctions regime: a profound rejection of the way in which basic features of the international economic system, such as the US dollar, the banking system and the internet, are being weaponized against whomever happens to disagree with current Western policies.
(5) Normative: a growing discontent with the emergence of a set of international rules and disciplines put forward by the developed countries, notably the US, whose effect is to

constrain the ability of governments to define and implement domestic policies.

The geopolitical differences between the developed North and the Global South have emerged starkly in the cases of the wars in Ukraine and Gaza, discussed in previous chapters. In relation to them, Western hypocrisy and double standards – in particular the differences in the Western reaction to the suffering of Ukrainians due to the Russian invasion, and that of the Palestinians because of Israel's attack on Gaza – have been blatant.

Beyond the efforts of Global South countries to end these tragic wars, something in which countries like Brazil and South Africa have taken a leading (albeit unsuccessful) role, the broader concern across the developing world is about the functioning (or lack thereof) of an international system that is no longer fit for purpose. Key pieces of that system are, of course, international organizations and the role they play in matters of war and peace, as well as in economic development.

Two entities are at the center of these concerns. One is the United Nations and especially the UN Security Council; the other, the Bretton Woods institutions, that is, the International Monetary Fund and the World Bank. The UNSC is made up of fifteen members, five of them permanent (the so-called Permanent 5 [P-5]: the US, China, Russia, France and the UK), plus ten rotating ones that serve for two years at a time. This arrangement reflects the realities of the post-World War II international power distribution, but not those of the new century. The net result is that the P-5 states use the veto power that their privileged position provides them to further their own strategic interests, while those of the Global South get short shrift. The fact that Western Europe has two members among the P-5, while Africa and Latin America have none, speaks volumes of the inequities of the UNSC. And the degree to which the veto power of the permanent members has stood in the way of ending the wars in Ukraine and Gaza is testimony to the degree the UN system is hampered in fulfilling one of its principal tasks – that of promoting peace in a troubled world.

A case can be made that reforming the UNSC would be a Herculean task, as the P-5 are unlikely to give up their veto power, and adding more permanent members *with* veto power to make the body more representative would make it even more dysfunctional – while adding them *without* veto power would place these new members in an unacceptable second-class category. A more promising avenue for change might thus be the Bretton Woods institutions. For long, both the World Bank and the IMF have been seen by developing countries as tools used by the developed nations to impose their own preferred economic policies and models on the rest of the world, generating much resentment. As in the UN, the US enjoys veto power in both institutions. Curiously, however, in one aspect of Bretton Woods institution reform, the road to change should be quite easy, at least from a purely legal point of view.

From the very beginning, an unwritten rule has been that the President of the World Bank should be a US citizen, and the Managing Director of the IMF should be a European (preferably French). Over the years, candidates vying for these positions (especially in the case of the IMF) have held out the promise that "next time it will be different," and that candidates from other nationalities would be considered, but it has never happened. No charter reforms and no special legislation in the member countries would be needed to implement a change that would allow, for the first time, citizens from Global South countries to run the World Bank and the IMF – though whether this would happen, given the political currents in the US and in Europe, is a different matter. A separate issue is that of the weighted quota governance system in both institutions, which also bears little relation to present economic realities. This gives inordinate powers to developed nations, and is also something that needs urgent reform.

Trade, investment and finance

The upsurge of the Global South on the geopolitical front has gone together with its economic rise. A key factor in this has been China. According to the IMF, in 2024 China had a GDP in purchasing power parity terms that was 28.3 percent larger than that of the US. Other indicators are no less telling. South-South trade as a share of global trade rose from 17 percent in 2005 to 28 percent in 2021. South-South trade represented more than half of the trade of developing country regions, ranging from about 45 percent in Latin America to over 65 percent in South Asia and East Asia. A significant proportion of this represents trade with China, amounting to at least one fifth of all South-South trade flows across all developing country regions.[14]

China is now Africa's main trading partner, with a trade volume of $254 billion in 2021, a 35 percent year-on-year increase. In 2021, India-Africa trade reached $89.5 billion, a 60 percent year-on-year increase.[15] China is also the main trading partner of South America, with $485 billion of trade with Latin America as a whole.

The Global South has also become a major source of international investment. The outflow stock of FDI of

Table 7.2 Developing countries' FDI outward stock (millions of USD)

	2000	2010	2022	2023	Annual Growth
Total	668,288	2,903,474	9,391,648	9,976,074	12.47%
China	27,768	317,211	2,754,810	2,939,100	22.48%
India	1,733	96,901	222,628	235,956	11.85%
South Africa	27,328	83,249	207,954	157,764	7.92.%

Source: Authors' table based on data from the United Nations Trade and Development Organization, World Investment Report 2024, Annex, Table 2, pp. 160–2, https://unctad.org/publication/world-investment-report-2024.

developing economies went up from $668.2 million in 2000 to $9.976 billion in 2023, an annual growth of nearly 12.4 percent.[16]

The newly acquired weight of the Global South underscores its efforts at reforming the international economic and financial architecture to allow for a greater presence of developing nations. But this is not just limited to the economic sphere. It also includes the normative one.

Norms and disciplines of the rules-based order

References to the international rules-based order (RBO) – along the lines of "we reaffirm our resolve to uphold the international rules-based order where countries are free from all forms of military, economic and political coercion"[17] – are common in statements by Western powers and other nations. As noted in Chapter 1, it was repeatedly invoked in efforts to assemble a worldwide coalition against Russia after the latter's invasion of Ukraine, on the strength of the argument that, in so doing, Russia was threatening the very fabric of the RBO. Yet, it has been noted that "the growing popularity of the RBO has not always brought greater clarity as to what this concept entails. A clear definition of the RBO does not exist."[18]

John Ikenberry has proposed a definition of the open RBO as a set of commitments by states to operate according to principles, rules and institutions that provide governance that is not simply dictated by who is most powerful.[19] He adds that it comes in four layers:

- The basic concept of state sovereignty
- The treaties and institutions culminating in the United Nations system

- The work-oriented rules and institutions that came out of World War II, regulating interdependence: the IMF, the World Bank, the WHO
- A kind of Western liberal democracy component

On this last point Ikenberry adds: "You have the old democratic stakeholders who placed themselves in a kind of organizing position as the kind of patrons and curators of a system where we have gone beyond what existed in earlier eras . . . So its's not entirely wrong to say that American hegemony is at play." Another analyst goes further to suggest that, according to US and Australian interpretations, US primacy and its military alliances in the Asia-Pacific are part of their understanding of the RBO, which they claim has existed for more than six decades.[20]

In principle, it is difficult to object to the notion of a rules-based order equal for all. In practice, it does not quite work that way. Why should the Russian invasion of Ukraine be considered a violation of the RBO, but the US invasion of Iraq not? The objection of many Global South countries to the RBO is that it is, in effect, an instrument to further the interests of the West and of their transnational corporations. The refusal of the US to acknowledge that Israel has violated international humanitarian law in the war it wages in Gaza, despite overwhelming evidence to the contrary, is the clearest example of the double standard that, in the eyes of the Global South, Western powers employ when it comes to these rules.

Still, the matter goes beyond what might be called a selective application of the supposedly sacrosanct rules of this order, depending on whether the infraction is made by friend or foe. The rules themselves are increasingly being designed to limit the ability of governments to adopt and implement their own economic and political models. China has been particularly vocal in its criticism of this practice, especially in matters concerning global economic governance in the context of the World Trade Organization, a major component of the RBO.

Another area of the RBO that has come up for strong criticism on the part of Global South countries is that of the governance of international investment, in particular the system of Investor-State Dispute Settlement (ISDS). This is a procedure whereby foreign investors are entitled to sue governments before arbitration panels to demand compensation for policies or actions that could have a negative impact on their profitability, provided they contravene the principle of fair and equitable treatment. The principle has not been defined authoritatively and is therefore left to the discretion of the arbiters in each case. The system is administered by the World Bank's International Center for the Settlement of Investment Disputes (ICSID), but the arbiters are *ad hoc* and often international lawyers who take part in other cases representing corporations. The system has become a standard feature of bilateral trade and investment agreements.

Several Global South countries have opted out of the system, which has been criticized even by the EU. Neither Brazil nor South Africa are members of the ICSID, and India has produced a Model Trade Treaty to replace the bilateral agreements. This maintains the ISDS system but requires the investor to spend five years pursuing the claim in domestic courts before being able to go to international arbitration. This is consistent with the fact that India, while accepting the notion of an RBO, maintains that it is not something that already exists, but rather a project that must be developed. Bolivia, Ecuador and Indonesia have also terminated their existing bilateral agreements that subjected them to the ISDS.

The BRICS+ and the rise of the Global South

If there is one entity that epitomizes the higher profile of rising powers and emerging economies in this new world order, it is the BRICS+ group that came into its own in 2023, at the 15th

BRICS Summit held in Johannesburg, South Africa.[21] If until 2023 the BRICS summits had received scant coverage in the Western media, this was not the case with the Johannesburg summit. The reason for this was the announced expansion of the BRICS, the first since South Africa joined in 2010.

What is the BRICS group and where is it coming from?

With its first summit held in Yekaterinburg in 2009 (when it was still known as BRIC), and bringing together Brazil, Russia, India, China and South Africa, this informal group is emblematic of the New South that has arisen in the new century. Formed by a small group of countries with large territories and populations, each of which plays a key role in its respective regions, its summits have been held uninterruptedly since 2009 – an important test of the resilience and staying power of such groups.[22] In a revealing episode, as a presidential candidate in 2018, Jair Bolsonaro vowed that under his government Brazil would leave BRICS, as he considered it to be an anti-American entity. Yet, once in office, not only did he backtrack on that promise, but went as far as to host the 11th BRICS Summit in Brasília in November of 2019. He had to give in to the pressure of both the military and the business community, adamantly opposed to Brazil's leaving the group, one that enhances Brazil's standing in international affairs, providing it with regular access, at the highest level, to decision-makers in some of the world's largest and most influential nations.

From the very beginning, the BRICS group was subject to heavy criticism from Western media, because of the heterogeneity of its membership and the fact that it is formed by countries with very different political and economic systems.[23] Russia's membership was singled out for particular criticism, on the strength of the argument that it was not an "emerging power" but a "declining" one, and therefore had no right to be in the group at all, ignoring the role of agency and purpose in foreign policy, and the fact that the Russian Federation is the successor state to a former superpower, the Soviet Union. Another common criticism of the group was that it was nothing but a "talking-shop," good at releasing fancy declarations, but with little to show in terms of material support to back them up.[24] This came to an end in 2015 with the establishment by the BRICS of the New Development Bank (the so-called BRICS Bank). Headquartered in Shanghai, and with a capital of $50 billion, the NDB has been well evaluated by the credit agencies so far.

However that may be, the BRICS group, despite its internal differences (the most salient of which is the one between China and India, who have a longstanding border-dispute in the Himalayas), continued to go from strength to strength. When, in 2022, it was announced that the group was open to new members, some twenty countries applied to join. Six of them were accepted in Johannesburg in 2023: Argentina, Egypt, Ethiopia, Iran, Saudi Arabia and United Arab Emirates (UAE). If in 2023 the combined GDP, in PPP terms, of the five original BRICS countries was already higher than that of the G7, with these additions the BRICS will be an even bigger force to be reckoned with in world affairs: on 2024 forecasts, the BRICS+ group will represent 46 percent of the world's population; 38 percent of the world's GDP; 23 percent of exports; and 43 percent of oil production.[25] In contrast, the G7 countries, though rich, represent less than 10 percent of the world's population. The huge foreign exchange reserves of Saudi Arabia and the UAE point to a potential capital expansion of the NDB, which might catapult it into the frontlines of multilateral development banks.

None of this means that BRICS expansion will be a smooth process.[26] Argentina's new government declined the invitation to join, and Saudi Arabia is still mulling it over. Apart from the China-India border dispute (which may have led to President Xi's non-attendance at the G20 Summit in New Delhi in September 2023), there are also other differences among the members. China and Russia would seem to favor building the BRICS into an alternative to the G7, NATO and other Western alliances. India, Brazil and South Africa, on the other hand (which, not coincidentally, are also part of the India-Brazil-South Africa Initiative, that has been somewhat dormant in recent years),[27] are inclined towards a non-aligned stance for the group, one that would not embrace an anti-Western position, but instead pick and choose among the various issues and decide accordingly – much along the lines of ANA. That said, there is little doubt that the BRICS+ group has come into its own and casts a significant shadow over the international scenario. Its interest in looking for ways to develop alternatives to the USD as the international currency of choice have drawn particular attention, though this may be more of a medium-to-long-term project, and for now the emphasis has been on efforts to rely on the national currencies of the member states for any trade among themselves. In that regard, China's currency, the yuan (or RMB in its international version), is well positioned to make some inroads, which takes us to the broader (and not fully resolved) issue of the relationship between China and the Global South.

China in the Global South

A key question that needs to be confronted is that of the relationship between China and the Global South. On the one hand, China today is the second largest economy in the world, representing 19.2 percent of global GDP. On the other hand, its per capita income, at $12,758, is still lower than that of Latin America ($18,560) and that of the global average ($20,271). China itself claims that it is part of the developing world, and labels many of its foreign trade, investment and financial cooperation projects as South-South cooperation.

So, which is it? Is China part of the Global South or not?

The truth is that, from the very beginning, the relationship between China and the rest of the developing world has been ambiguous. Chinese Premier Zhou Enlai attended the 1955 Bandung Conference, and the Panchsheel foreign policy principles that Zhou worked out with Indian Prime Minister Jawaharlal Nehru to guide relations between China and India became guiding principles for the NAM. Yet, in keeping with the traditions of the Middle Kingdom, China was never *part* of the NAM, though it was associated with it as an observer. And while the G77 at the UN includes China in its list of members, the Chinese government prefers the name "Group of 77 and China," though it takes part in all the group's activities and negotiations.

As indicated above, China continues to call itself a developing country and refers to many of its economic activities abroad as "South-South cooperation," though for others at least some of those activities would better be described as straightforward business propositions. In turn, there is no doubt that China has been a driving force behind the emergence of the Global South as a credible economic actor, with initiatives like the Asian Investment and Infrastructure Bank, the NDB and the Belt and Road Initiative, that have brought greater pluralism and diversity to the until now largely Western-dominated scene of international financial institutions (IFIs) and development lending.

On the other hand, China cannot have it both ways. From a strictly institutional perspective, the fact that China does not consider itself part of the NAM or of the G77 at the United Nations is a telling indicator that it does not see itself as part of the Global South, despite occasional protestations to the contrary.[28] From a developmentalist perspective, one could make the argument that, despite its still middling per capita income, given the sheer size of its economy and its enormous progress, China has already "graduated" from its condition as a developing country and now stands on its own.

China's rejection of the West's attempt to instrumentalize the RBO to impose the neoliberal capitalist model on the

Global South is consistent with the fact that it does not seek to impose its own model – economic or political – on others. Empirical studies have shown no correlation between Chinese international trade and the similarity, or lack thereof, between the Chinese government system and that of its partners. They do show, however, that in the field of international cooperation there is a strong correlation between the amount of aid China provides and the support of the beneficiaries of that aid for China's foreign policy objectives, especially on issues like Taiwan and Tibet.

In the area of international investment, the picture is more nuanced. China maintains that there is a fundamental difference between its investments (and foreign aid) and those of the developed capitalist countries. This has led some observers to herald the emergence of a "Beijing Consensus" as an alternative to the Washington Consensus.[29] The Chinese approach involves no-strings-attached financing, often interest-free or nominal interest rates, with the possibility of payments in natural resources and without conditionality clauses such as those imposed by the World Bank.

Still, analysts and especially non-governmental organizations (NGOs) and some governments have criticized other aspects of Chinese international investment policy, including things like lending beyond the repayment capability of the borrower; crowding out local production through massive exports into the local market; crowding out local manpower by bringing in crews of Chinese workers; land-grabbing, especially in Africa; and disregard for the impact of projects on the environment, local communities and human rights, especially in Latin America. Various studies have shown that many of these criticisms are unfounded, but not all.[30] In Latin America, issues related to the environment and the rights of indigenous communities have been real enough. China has generally been willing to meet the concerns of Global South countries in these matters.

China's position and interests as a major capital exporter have become apparent in its approach to some key aspects of the international governance of investments. China participated actively in the work on a multilateral framework on investment facilitation at the WTO, started in 2017. In doing this, China abandoned its traditional opposition to the inclusion of investment among WTO disciplines, even though the terms of reference of the discussions – partly due to Chinese pressure – indicated they would focus on improving transparency, streamlining procedures and improving the exchange of information, and specifically excluded the issues of market access and investor-state dispute settlement.

However, a large number of countries, led by India and South Africa (China's BRICS partners), opposed the proposal.[31] In addition to objections to the legal bases of the proposal, this was done because it is difficult to separate the issue of facilitation from those of investment protection and access for foreign investors to domestic markets. Thus, an eventual facilitation agreement would inevitably interfere with the ability of states to select investments, and open the door to the liberalization of FDI flows and the unbridled penetration of transnational capital into developing economies.

A second issue on which China has distanced itself from leading Global South countries is that of the system for the settlement of investment disputes. As indicated above, a growing number of developing nations are dissatisfied with the current ISDS arrangements managed by the ICSID of the World Bank. China, however, has not raised substantive objections to the system, although it has proposed a set of changes to its rules.[32] They are for the most part solely procedural, with the exception of a proposal to make the rules of interpretation of the Vienna Convention on the Law of Treaties mandatory, which does not fundamentally alter the way in which the system has worked so far; a proposal on conflict of interest, which does not deal with the essence of the problem; and one on cases

Table 7.3 ICSID: Chinese companies' demands for compensation

Year	Respondent State	Outcome
2007	Peru	In favor investor
2010	Mongolia	In favor State
2012	Belgium	In favor State
2014	Yemen	Settled
2017	Laos	Pending
2018	Nigeria	In favor investor
2019	Greece	Discontinued
2020	Korea	Pending
2021	Finland	Pending
2021	Ghana	In favor State
2021	Malta	Pending
2022	Vietnam	Pending
2022	Ecuador	Pending
2022	Sweden	Pending
2023	Vietnam	Pending
2023	Trinidad and Tobago	Pending

Source: Authors' table based on data from the United Nations Trade and Development Organization, Investment Policy Hub, China: Cases as Home State Claimant, https://investmentpolicy.unctad.org/investment-dispute-settlement/country/42/china/investor.

in which legal costs that have been covered by third parties should not be included in the costs to be allocated. In other words, China is basically comfortable with ISDS and ICSID, and proposes marginal changes to them. Moreover, Chinese investors have used the ISDS system regularly to try to extract compensation from developing nations, as Table 7.3 shows.

Another area where China is at odds with a substantial section of the Global South is that of human rights. This became apparent in September 2022 when the UN High Commissioner for Human Rights released a report on the human rights situation in the Xinjiang Uyghur Autonomous Region of China (XUAR), which found that "serious human rights violations have been committed in XUAR in the context of the Government's application of counter-terrorism and counter-'extremism' strategies," and that these violations "may constitute international crimes, in particular crimes against humanity."[33]

The report was rejected by the Chinese government in the strongest terms: "The 'assessment' based on presumption of guilt uses disinformation and lies fabricated by anti-China forces as its main sources, deliberately ignores authoritative information and objective materials provided by the Chinese government, maliciously distorts China's laws and policies."[34]

On September 26, the representative of Pakistan in the UN Human Rights Council delivered a joint statement on behalf of sixty-eight countries of the Global South, plus Russia, rejecting the report and supporting China. The signatory governments opposed the "politicization of human rights and double standards, or interference in China's internal affairs under the pretext of human rights." They called for respect for "the right of the people of each state to choose independently the path for development in accordance with their national conditions. All human rights should be treated with the same emphasis, with sufficient importance attached to economic, social and cultural rights and the right to development in particular."[35]

In a subsequent vote of the Council on a motion by the US and Norway to hold a debate on the report, the motion was rejected by nineteen votes to seventeen, with eleven abstentions. The Latin American countries who voted against holding a debate (i.e., in support of the Chinese position) were Bolivia, Cuba and Venezuela. Argentina, Brazil and Mexico abstained, as did India and Malaysia. The only Global South countries voting in favor of the motion were Honduras and Paraguay.[36] Yes, there are differences on the issue of human rights between China and many developing countries, but, as a rule, they are not allowed to get out of hand and spill over into key UN votes.

Conclusion

The Global South as an international actor has been described as "a space under construction," something that should be apparent from the above discussion.[37] There are significant differences among the countries in it. Yet, they also share certain common concerns that have triggered a dynamic in an international system in transition, one that is moving away from unbridled US hegemony towards what Amitav Acharya has described as a multiplex system in which power and influence are more widely distributed. Russia's invasion of Ukraine and the international fallout from it, as well as Hamas's attack on Israel and the subsequent Israeli response, bringing about tens of thousands of civilian deaths in Gaza, have brought to the fore the profound dissatisfaction of many countries in Africa, Asia and Latin America with Western double standards, as well as with the hypocrisy embodied in the much-heralded RBO. But this dissatisfaction goes way beyond these wars and the realities of selective compassion and disregard for basic principles of international law they have shown. The rise of the Global South is the product of a deep disillusionment with the way the current international system is operating, one that shows little regard for the many global challenges faced by a world in turmoil, while the Great Powers play their own one-upmanship games.

Under such circumstances, what does the Global South want? While the huge differences among Global South countries do not make it easy to articulate a common program, are there certain demands on which they coincide? If so, what are they? And to what extent does ANA provide a vehicle to channel these demands? Is ANA more of a transactional approach to foreign policy, one that lends itself to the day-to-day management of diplomatic affairs rather than to the more ambitious undertaking of conceptualizing, proposing and executing major global governance reforms? These are the questions to which we now turn in the final chapter of this book.

Conclusion

In May 2024, the ICC prosecutor Kiram Khan announced that he would seek arrest warrants for Hamas leaders Yayha Sinwar, Mohammed Diab Ibrahim al-Masri and Ismail Haniyeh for war crimes and crimes against humanity committed in the attack on Israel on October 7, 2023. Concurrently, he also sought arrest warrants for the Israeli Prime Minister Benjamin Netanyahu and Israel's Defense Minister Yoav Gallant for the ensuing attack by Israel on Gaza.[1]

On the face of it, this seemed like a fair and balanced response to the tragic conflict in Gaza that has led to so much suffering and to so many casualties on both sides. Yet, it was immediately denounced by the US government as unacceptable, an act engaging in a "false equivalence" by equating the actions of a terrorist group like Hamas with those of a democratic state like Israel.[2] US Republican Senators – who had threatened Mr. Khan in advance, warning him that any such action would bring a swift retaliation on the part of the US government, imposing sanctions not only on him but also on his family and the rest of the ICC staff – immediately called for the application of such sanctions.[3] Secretary of State Antony Blinken agreed with such calls, and expressed his desire to work together with the legislators to impose sanctions on the ICC.[4]

This was not the first time the US had enacted sanctions against the ICC, of which it is not a member; it had already done so in 2020 under the first Trump administration, in response to an initiative of Mr. Khan's predecessor, Ms. Fatou Bensouda, to investigate alleged war crimes committed in Afghanistan by US military personnel.[5] But it does underscore the remarkable double standard applied by Western powers when it comes to matters of international law. In 2022, the US worked closely with the ICC to facilitate the issuance of an arrest warrant against Russian President Vladimir Putin for alleged war crimes committed in the war in Ukraine,[6] a war in which far fewer women and children have died in two years than in four months in the war in Gaza.[7] Suddenly, in relation to Gaza, Washington's argument was that the ICC has no jurisdiction because Israel is not a member (neither is Russia).

It is one thing to argue that the ICC has no jurisdiction in this case. It is quite another to enact sanctions against an international court simply because one disagrees with its actions, and to do so not just in reaction to measures taken against your own citizens, but in reaction to measures affecting a third party.

The fact that this was undertaken by the world's leading power and self-proclaimed champion of the so-called rules-based order only underscores the degree to which this order is crumbling before our very eyes. If an RBO is not about accepting the rulings of international courts, what is it about? This also explains why more and more countries across the Global South are striking out, embracing non-alignment and expressing their deep skepticism of an order that seems to many to be nothing but a smokescreen for Western strategic interests – in this case, to defend Israel, the West's prime ally in the Middle East, come what may.

Sanctions and economic warfare

Enacting sanctions against an international court and its staff because it takes measures you disagree with might strike some as the height of absurdity (what comes next? bombing The Hague?), but it only takes to its logical conclusion a trend that has emerged over the past two decades.[8] As Farrell and Newman point out in their book, *Underground Empire: How America Weaponized the World Economy*, the US has managed to deploy its *de facto* control of internet governance and the international banking system, and the hegemony of the US dollar, not just against its adversaries, but against anybody Washington happens to disagree with. Thus, "Trump's administration used the power of the US financial system, for example, to target not just terrorists, but human rights officials."[9]

The use of economic sanctions has thus become not a measure of last resort for Washington, but of first resort. It also comes with a particular twist. Sanctions give the officials who enact them a certain virtuous feeling, because they fall short of military action. In fact, of course, "they are signals of antagonism and cost imposition, sometimes equated to acts of war themselves."[10] Not surprisingly, as we saw in Chapter 1, though the vast majority of countries in the Global South condemned the Russian invasion of Ukraine, the overwhelming majority also rejected the imposition of unilateral Western sanctions on Russia.

If the international banking system, the US dollar and the internet are regarded by states as the equivalent of what citizens regard as utility systems at home, weaponizing them cannot but arouse deep resentment on the part of weaker states, who see themselves at the receiving end of this economic warfare through sanctions. And that is why ANA argues for monetary pluralism, as mentioned in Chapter 4. It is the dollar's hegemony that gives the US the ability to impose these sanctions – hence the calls for a more diversified basket of currencies to provide greater stability and predictability in international economic affairs.

An era in flux and the rise of the Global South

Sanctions have thus evolved into the primary form of waging economic warfare in the new century. According to some estimates, 30 percent of the world's population lives in countries affected by them, with all the consequences that entails.[11] In turn, sanctions are an expression of the broader trend we discussed in Chapter 7, as the world shifts from the age of globalization to one of fragmentation, one in which geopolitics replaces geoeconomics as the key driver of international affairs. Terms like "nearshoring" and "friendshoring" for investment locations reflect the degree to which ideology rather than economic efficiency has become a criterion for what used to be strictly commercial decisions.

What Gramsci referred to as the "interregnum" – the moment of crisis in which the old is dying but the new is not yet born, and all sorts of maladies arise – is in full swing. The transition from the unipolar moment that followed the end of the Cold War to that of the Great Power competition we are seeing today, mostly between the United States and China, but also between the US and Russia, is one expression of it. Deglobalization is another, one that goes together with the rise of populism, protectionism and isolationism in the West – of which strong anti-immigrant sentiments are a key component.[12] All of this has led to the slow but steady dismantling of the liberal international order erected in the aftermath of World War II, based on principles such as free trade and multilateralism, now abandoned by their erstwhile champions like the US and the UK, presently absorbed by their own internal problems.

The rise of the Global South and its contestation of the current world order takes place in this context. Although the term is not uncontroversial, and some question its supposed imprecision, it refers to the 134 countries that form the G77 group at the United Nations, mostly from Africa, Asia and Latin America. These countries are unhappy with current international arrangements, which they feel are stacked against them, both politically and economically. It is a diverse group – some of them are middle powers that exercise a certain degree of influence, while others are very small and/or very poor – and they do not necessarily agree on a detailed common program. Yet, they share a sense of grievance against a system that they feel is not responsive to the needs of most of the world's population and has not been for a long time. As one reporter put it: "With inequality worsening, food security worsening, energy security worsening and climate change accelerating, more countries are asking what answers the post-1945 Western-dominated order can provide."[13] Yes, members of the Global South do have very different political and economic systems, ideologies and levels of development, though most of them share a colonial past. Yet, they converge in the sentiment that they have been excluded from the high table of world politics and would like to change that.

This sentiment has been accentuated by the growth of Great Power competition from 2018 onwards, in what many developing nations consider to be the petty one-upmanship between Washington and Beijing, and the concomitant pressures on these nations to take sides in this struggle for primacy in world affairs. While the main concern for the weaker states in Africa, Asia and Latin America is development, they keep being pressured to take sides in grandiose ideological contests that have little to do with lifting their populations out of poverty and destitution, which is the key priority of their governments. Still, however challenging this predicament may be, it also offers an opportunity, one that was not available in the years of the Cold War, nor in those of unquestioned US hegemony.

The current era, then, is marked by two key phenomena. One is the return of Great Power competition to world affairs. The other is the Global South's contestation, however inchoate and tentative, of the current world order. Much will depend on the way they interact in years to come. If there is any truth to the saying "demography is destiny," then the fact that the G7 represents a mere 10 percent of the world's population and the Global Majority some 80 percent of it should tell us that the answer to how this will be resolved is by no means obvious. In this setting, what should the countries of the Global South do? Enter Active Non-Alignment.

ANA as the way forward

It is in this context of an international system in transition, in which might makes right and established rules have flown out the window, that ANA comes to the fore. It does so at a particularly perilous moment in world affairs, in which various factors converge to bring the very subsistence of humanity into question – thus the terms "polycrisis" or "permacrisis."[14] The fact that this period also bears the imprint of Great Power competition, one marked by the perceived decline of the hegemonic power and the rise of another, makes matters even more perilous. As Graham Allison has noted, historically these types of competition often end in war, sometimes even against the will of the warring parties.[15] Whether this will also hold in the nuclear age, with all the consequences that entails, remains to be seen. But there is little doubt that the present era can well be described as an Age of Uncertainty.

Under these circumstances, ANA has gained traction across the Global South for two reasons: a) as a correct *diagnosis* of the international situation; and b) as a *guide to action* to overcome present-day challenges. Embracing it, as the South African government has formally done,[16] means leaving behind the laments and self-victimization of the *diplomatie des cahiers de doléances* of yesteryear and opening the way to initiatives designed to change the current international order, which has long ceased to respond to the realities and imperatives of our time. The financial crisis of 2008–9 (which led to the establishment of the G20, as the G7 was unable to handle it on its own); the COVID-19 pandemic – the worst in a century, thoroughly mismanaged at the multilateral level, and exposing the self-centeredness of the US and Europe as they embraced vaccine nationalism, ignoring the requirements of the rest of the world; the extraordinary case of NATO, a military alliance whose original purpose vanished many years ago and that now "largely exists to manage the risks created by its own existence";[17] the war in Gaza, which has exposed the hollowness of the West's self-description as a champion of human rights; and the widespread consensus that the Millennium Development Goals (MDGs) will not be reached by 2030 – all are symptoms of this larger malaise affecting the existing world order, "an age of chaos" in the words of UN Secretary-General António Guterres.[18]

The Great Powers have shown a stubborn unwillingness to take steps towards adjusting the extant architecture of global governance to the current realities on the ground. Under such circumstances, it is easy for most states, which tend to be post-colonial, developing, weaker states, to be imbued with a sense of despair. Yet, as has been discussed in this book, the rise of the Global South as a new actor on the international scene can give a new impetus to longstanding efforts to reshape this world order. In turn, Active Non-Alignment is the natural foreign policy choice for developing nations, one that also acts as a centrifugal force in bringing together under a common roof (if not necessarily on a common platform) countries from Africa, Asia and Latin America.

As Tom Long has shown, even quite small states can make a difference in world affairs and move the needle in their preferred direction.[19] Yes, small need not only be beautiful, it can also be influential. Our argument in this book has been that the current international configuration, despite its inherent perils, is one that lends itself especially to a particular approach to foreign policy, one that we have called Active Non-Alignment.

One criticism of this approach, echoing the views of US Secretary of State John Foster Dulles on non-alignment in the 1950s, is that it is "immoral," as it would fail to distinguish between "good and evil." Yet, as we discussed in Chapter 2, the issue of "values" has many angles, and a proper response to what each of them entails is by no means straightforward. On the one hand, countries like the United States have very little credibility when it comes to upholding democratic values abroad, since, as Steven Cook has put it, "loving dictators is as American as apple pie."[20] On the other hand, the harsh reality is that for weak states in today's world the main imperative is development and the welfare of their population. The notion that their economic progress and growth should be sacrificed for the sake of a supposedly shared commitment to certain abstract values aligned with one or another of the Great Powers finds little purchase in most developing countries today. This is particularly true given that the Great Powers themselves have no objection to sacrificing those much-vaunted values to their own strategic objectives, as the case of Gaza so painfully shows. Far from reflecting a policy of mere opportunism, as is sometimes alleged, ANA embodies simply the best strategy to deal with an uncertain and perilous environment.

In the current Great Power competition between the US and China, both Washington and Beijing feel impelled to vie for "the hearts and minds" of countries around the world. In the case of the US, this is to prove that its hegemonic status is not declining; in the case of China, to show that its own standing continues to rise. This opens considerable opportunities for weaker states "to play the field," in Kassab's apt expression, and make the most of what that entails.[21] This opening did not obtain during the Cold War, or, if it did, it was to a much lesser degree, given the small size of the Soviet economy. Neither did it obtain during the "unipolar moment" of undisputed US hegemony after the end of the Cold War.

Instead of raising their arms in despair because of the "polycrisis," many countries in Africa, Asia and Latin America are taking advantage of this Great Power competition and leveraging it for their own purposes. President William Ruto of Kenya visits China in 2023 to lobby for an expansion of China's railway projects in his country, and shortly thereafter visits Washington, the first African head of state since 2008 to be offered a state dinner in the White House, and the first Kenyan President to do so since the Carter presidency. There, he is given the royal treatment, as he commits to deploy a Kenyan police force to pacify a gang-controlled Haiti.[22]

President Lula of Brazil, who has a strong rapport both with President Biden and with President Xi, works closely with the US on climate change issues, but on issues like the wars in Ukraine and in Gaza, his stance is closer to China's.[23] Prime Minister Narendra Modi has made India part of the Quad – a strategic dialogue that includes the US, and is sometimes referred to as an "Asian NATO" – but has also refused to condemn the Russian invasion of Ukraine, and has no objection to undertaking a state visit to Russia at the height of the war. India has also considerably increased its purchases of Russian oil (albeit at a steep discount), providing Russia with a much-needed source of foreign exchange, after the decline in Russian gas and oil sales to Europe in the wake of its invasion of Ukraine.[24]

ASEAN, considered by some as one of the most successful cases of regional integration anywhere, has also managed to position itself as a significant diplomatic interlocutor to the Great Powers precisely by asserting its non-aligned stance; the group is in many ways Exhibit A of the advantages that ensue from such an approach, as discussed in Chapter 5. Vietnam, described by the World Bank as a "development success" – transiting as it has from being one of the poorest countries in the world to a middle-income one in a mere forty years, among other things due to the application of "bamboo diplomacy" under the leadership of Nguyen Phu Trong (2011–24), an approach that shares much with ANA – is a shining example of the advantages accruing to nations willing to deploy non-alignment and to refuse binary choices in the management of their foreign relations.[25]

Many countries around the world, from Ecuador to South Africa, Chile to Indonesia, Vietnam to Peru, have followed a similar path, and benefited accordingly. By keeping their options open, considering various alternatives, playing their cards close to their vest and refusing to simply side with one or the other of the Great Powers – in other words, by hedging their bets in the face of uncertainty – they show not only that Great Power competition need not be an unsurmountable obstacle for weaker states to thrive, but that it actually offers real opportunities to do so. They are there for the taking.

The Global South, ANA and the way forward

As a recent report, "A Logic for the Future: International Relations in an Age of Turbulence,"[26] underscores, we find ourselves at one of those turning points in history, in which the accumulation of a variety of crises in terms of international conflicts, economic instability and natural disasters spurred by climate change has reached a nadir. As should be obvious, current international arrangements are no longer fit for purpose and require a major overhaul.

While a post-Western world may still be some decades away,[27] there is little doubt that Western powers, which have held sway in the international system for the past two centuries, are finding it increasingly difficult to provide the global public goods the world needs. Instead, they retreat into their own cocoons. This became especially apparent during the COVID-19 pandemic, as vaccine nationalism ran rampant in the United States and Europe, triggering their refusal to sell vaccines to countries in the Global South in the first half of 2021, despite the abundance of stocks – a choice that may have cost millions of lives. This retreat by the West from global responsibilities, this so-called "Westlessness,"[28] thus presents a huge challenge to the Global South and to Active Non-Alignment.

As we have discussed in this book, a key feature of ANA as a foreign policy doctrine has been its pragmatic, non-ideological, almost transactional character. ANA provides a compass to developing nations to navigate a troubled world, as it "plays the field" and relies on hedging in the management of foreign affairs. Less a movement than a certain approach to the conduct of foreign relations, it has shown that its tool kit comes in handy in the stormy weather of the second and third decades of the new century. Great Power competition and Global South contestation are signature features of this world in transition. Yet, the decline of the West and of the liberal international order, and the resulting international anomie (as reflected, for example, in the paralysis of the World Trade Organization – induced by the United States – and in the inability of Western governments to reign in Israel's bombing of civilians in Gaza), calls for a more ambitious agenda.

Given the planetary nature of these emerging challenges, and the inability of current structures to respond to them in any meaningful fashion, we would like to suggest that ANA will have to up its game and develop a more capacious agenda, one that reflects the unmet needs of the Global Majority. Reaching a consensus on any such program will not be easy, and neither will its enactment, however partial and tentative. But, under current circumstances, doing nothing is not an option. While the Global South has shown a remarkable degree of *convergence* on several issues, it is still far from displaying any sort of systematic *collective action* to further its goals. In our judgement, the latter should include the following:

1. *Revert deglobalization*
   After thirty-five years that brought much progress to humanity and lifted over a billion people out of poverty, since 2016 (the year the UK voted to leave the European Union and the US first elected Donald J. Trump to the presidency) the latest phase of globalization has come to an end and gone into reverse gear. From an ever more integrated and interdependent world economy we have moved to a steadily more fragmented one. Geopolitical rather than commercial considerations guide investment and trade decisions. The two biggest markets in the world, the United States and the European Union, embrace protectionism and reject the free trade principles they once championed. The WTO is paralyzed, unilateral economic sanctions rule the roost, and there is little concern with giving a new boost to international trade in goods. This is not to say that unbridled free trade is a panacea, but a non-functioning international trade rule-making body is not the answer either. What the world needs is a working system that monitors global trade; that provides a common but differentiated set of rules that govern it, taking into consideration the differences between developed and developed economies; that ends the inordinate subsidies to agriculture of developed countries that distort world markets; that introduces more flexible IP rules that make it easier for developing nations to deal with their own health and other needs; and that limits trade agreements to actual trade matters, without extending to "beyond the border" disciplines like SOEs, competition policy and government procurement.[29]

2. *Fight climate change*
   The year 2023 was the hottest on record, and across the world thousands of people are dying because of these high temperatures. More intense and more frequent hurricanes, typhoons and monsoons, as well as changes in maritime currents like El Niño, wreak havoc everywhere, and often disproportionally affect the Global South. The window for cutting carbon emissions before it is too late and the planet suffers irreversible damage is closing quickly, yet there is little sense of urgency in the Global North to do the needful. Its promise to contribute $100 billion a year to developing countries to cut emissions remains an empty one, whereas the war in Ukraine quickly triggered $200 billion in aid from the US and Europe in a scarce two years – a stark reminder that the issue is not one of availability of resources, but rather of political will and foreign policy priorities. This is above all a joint, global task, but the fact that in some developed countries the very words "climate change" are being scrubbed from official documents is revealing of the climate change denialism that exists, and that makes it so much harder to address what some consider to be the most serious threat facing humanity.

3. *Reform multilateral institutions*
   The notion that eighty years after the end of World War II and the establishment of the United Nations there are still two mid-sized Western European states as permanent members of the UN Security Council, but no African or Latin American member states in that category, strikes many as a curious anomaly, the equivalent of a contemporary postal service using horse-drawn carriages to deliver the mail. Yet, that is where we are. In the case of the Bretton Woods institutions – the World Bank and the IMF – much the same goes for the unwritten rule that the head of the first must be a US citizen and the head

of the latter a European one, preferably a Frenchman or woman. How much time must elapse before these anachronistic rules and practices favoring the victors of World War II are ended? A full century? Voting shares in these IFIs have also long failed to represent the respective sizes of the membership, giving the US a de facto veto in both, only adding to the distrust they elicit in much of the Global South. Not surprisingly, the legitimacy of these institutions is strongly questioned across the developing world. A UNSC that truly reflects the realities on the ground in today's world, and IFIs with voting rights that do the same, with IMF Special Drawing Rights that are allocated more fairly (rather than with a skewed formula that benefits the richest countries), should be on the agenda, as well as the establishment of the principle of one member state, one vote in IFIs.

4. *Prioritize development*
As Richard Gowan has pointed out,[30] as Global South UN member states geared up for the Summit of the Future held in New York City in September 2024, they underscored the need to put development front and center on the UN's agenda. Financial indebtedness is a huge issue in many countries across the South, from Ecuador to Ghana, Argentina to Zambia, and Kenya to Sri Lanka, yet their sense is that their predicament does not resonate in the capitals of the Great Powers. These seem more concerned with competing with each other than listening to and acting on the troubles and travails of the Great Majority. Revealingly, at this point there is a consensus that the 2030 MDGs will not be achieved. Debt relief, facilitating greater access to developed country markets by developing countries, and putting human wellbeing at the center of sustainable development – as opposed to giving free reign to the forces of demand and supply – should guide such an approach.

5. *Foster greater equality*
   The 1980–2016 so-called third wave of globalization was very effective in reducing poverty, especially in China and India, but also elsewhere, dispensing with the myth that globalization would only favor the rich countries. In fact, part of the populist reaction against everything foreign that can be seen in several Northern nations, most prominently in the US and the UK, but also elsewhere, can be traced back to a sense that countries like China and India have taken good factory jobs away from places like Detroit and Manchester. In the US there is even a verb for it: "to be Bangalored" – referring to someone who lost his or her job because it was transferred to Bangalore in Southern India, also known as "India's Silicon Valley."

   What globalization was less effective at was reducing inequality – in fact it may have increased it. Not surprisingly, the mass migrations that we witness today are triggered not just by the population displacement caused by war and natural disasters, but also by the demonstration effect of life in the rich countries of the Global North, images of which are conveyed daily to the rest of the planet via ubiquitous social media. In the delicate balancing act entailed in making the most of the virtues of the market while nudging and pushing it in the right direction via suitable public policies, the neoliberal emphasis has been on policies that promote growth, often at all costs. Equality needs to be put back into the public policy mix, both internationally and nationally, if the dystopian future so many projected scenarios contemplate is to be avoided.

* * *

The Battle of Cuito Cuanavale, fought in Southern Angola from August 1987 to March 1988, was the largest battle fought in Africa since World War II. It marked a turning point in the denouement of the Cold War in Africa. Pitting the forces of the

MPLA-led Angolan government, with the support of Cuban brigades and Soviet advisors, against those of the UNITA rebels, led by Jonas Savimbi, supported by South African forces and armed by the US, its outcome brought about the independence of Namibia, the end of the apartheid regime in South Africa and the consolidation of MPLA rule in Angola – a country rich in oil, diamonds and so much fertile land that it could feed all of Africa. Almost forty years later, the MPLA is still in power, but the country's immense natural riches have not percolated to the average Angolan, as more than one third of the population of 38 million still lives below the poverty line.

What has not changed, though, is the critical place Angola once again occupies in Great Power competition, though this time with slightly different players than during the Cold War. Over the past fifteen years or so, the Angolan government has relied heavily on Chinese loans and investment to build infrastructure, invest in mining and agriculture and otherwise contribute to economic progress, making it the biggest recipient of Chinese financing in the continent, to the tune of some $45 billion. Yet, due to chronic corruption and lack of state capacity, Angola has been unable to translate this into sustained economic growth. Enter the US. To diversify his country's foreign links, President João Lourenço (2017–) has reached out to Washington to bring fresh capital and new ideas to Angola's development challenges.

To the surprise of many, this has led to US involvement in what is the largest railway project in Africa today, the Lobito Corridor, building on the existing lines of the Benguela Railway Company, which go back all the way to 1902, but were badly damaged during the Angolan civil war. A $10 billion project, the plan is for the Lobito Corridor to run from Kolwezi in the Democratic Republic of Congo (DRC) to Angola's Lobito port on the Atlantic coast, before possibly being extended all the way to Zambia. This would cut transport time to port for the copper and other mineral riches of the DRC by more than three fourths, to five–seven days, from the thirty–thirty-five days it currently takes by road to the Indian Ocean ports of Dar es Salaam in Tanzania, Beira in Mozambique or Durban in South Africa. Deploying the G7's Partnership for Global Infrastructure and Investment – the group's answer to China's Belt and Road Initiative – the US International Development Finance Corporation has committed $553 million to the renewal of the Angolan railway line. The Lobito Atlantic Railway predicts it will carry 200,000 tons of minerals in 2024 but aims to transport 2 million tons in years to come, not too far from the 3 million tons the Benguela Railway Company used to carry in its heyday, before Angolan independence.[31]

Ten years ago, the notion that the US – the land that worships the automobile and has difficulty keeping its own creaking railway system in working condition – would be in the business of financing a 1,716 km railway in Southern Africa would have been dismissed as downright fanciful, if not as sheer lunacy. Yet today it is very much a reality. And the reasons for it are not difficult to fathom. Much as it has in Latin America, China has made considerable inroads in Africa in the new century, both on the trade and investment fronts. In 2023, trade between China and Africa reached $281 billion, whereas US-Africa trade was less than one fourth of that, at $67.5 billion. Since 2000, it is estimated that China has lent some $170 billion to Africa for various projects.[32] Not surprisingly, the US is keen to catch up. As one former US official put it, commenting on the Lobito Corridor: "There is no denying this is a response to the Belt and Road."[33]

Much must happen before the Lobito Corridor is fully in place, and it remains to be seen whether it will ever fulfill its considerable promise. But the launch of this ambitious project by Angola – China's biggest loan recipient in Africa – and Luanda's reaching out to the G7 and the US to materialize it, is emblematic of our time and of how developing nations are managing Great Power competition. It reflects the refusal by

African countries to align themselves with one or another of the Great Powers, as well as their willingness to hedge their bets and play both sides against the middle. As one observer put it: "Angola is doing the smart thing many African countries are now doing: they want to be friends with everyone, but they don't want to be owned by anyone."[34]

In many ways, this is what Active Non-Alignment is all about.

Afterword

As this book was about to go to press, the reelection of Donald J. Trump to a second (non-consecutive) term on November 5, 2024 raised new questions about the direction the transition to a different world order will take. The same goes for the ensuing Great Power competition between the United States and China, and its impact on Active Non-Alignment as an approach to the foreign policy of developing states. ANA arose in 2019–20, during President Trump's first term, in response to his administration's pressure on Latin American governments to cancel projects associated with China and otherwise curtail business with Beijing. This came at a time of the region's biggest economic downturn in 120 years, as well as that of a major health crisis, caused by the COVID-19 pandemic.

What will be the effect of a second Trump administration's policies on Latin America and the Global South more generally?

To answer this question, we should keep in mind that the world is far more troubled in 2025 than it was in 2017. The existence of three major wars – in Ukraine, Gaza and Sudan; trade tensions arising from the tit-for-tat imposition of tariffs between the United States and China, as well as between the

European Union and China; and the ongoing stalemate over how to pay for the fight against climate change evidenced at the COP29 meeting in Baku, are only some of the factors reflecting a far more uncertain and volatile world than when Trump was first elected.[1]

And that first election was originally seen by many as a mere bump in the road in the long trajectory of American exceptionalism and the liberal international order the United States had established at the end of World War II. The latter was based on the principles of free trade, multilateralism, liberal democracy and Washington's leading role in the provision of global public goods. Yet, Trump's reelection, essentially a repudiation of all the above, would seem to indicate that that era is over and a new period is upon us, one in which the world's greatest power will play a very different role – one based on protectionism, unilateralism and a strong penchant for the values normally associated with authoritarianism and isolationism.

The degree to which the old verities about the management of international relations are being upended (and will be further upended in President-elect Trump's second term) is already apparent. He has thrown a spanner into the USMCA – the trade agreement between the US, Mexico and Canada that replaced NAFTA – that was negotiated in Trump's first term, but that he has never really liked. In November 2024 – and contrary to the traditional notion that the United States has one President at a time – Trump announced he would impose a 25 percent tariff on all goods coming into the United States from Canada and Mexico, and an extra 10 percent on goods coming from China.[2] Quite apart from what this would do to US-China trade (and what the ensuing retaliatory measures China would impose on US goods would do to the US economy), these tariffs would have a devastating impact on intra-regional USMCA trade – which represents 40 percent of all trade of the member countries. They would also have a major impact on the price of imported fruits and vegetables in the United States, many of which come from Mexico. But perhaps the most serious effect would be felt by the automobile industry, as auto parts cross borders back and forth many times.

The argument has been made that Trump is bluffing, or at least using such announcements merely as a negotiating tactic to extract concessions from the United States' three main trading partners.[3] That may well be the case. But these announcements have had a very real effect on state behavior and elicited a variety of reactions from international leaders. This gives us an inkling of what can be expected in interactions between the incoming Trump administration and the rest of the world in years to come. The case of Canada is an especially revealing one, as a close ally of the United States and one that has gone out of its way to accommodate US foreign policy priorities, even at considerable cost to itself.[4] The initial reaction in Ottawa was one of downright panic, with the leader of the opposition, Pierre Poilievre, suggesting that the best thing to do under the circumstances was to expel Mexico from the USMCA, leaving the latter with only the United States and Canada as members.[5] He rationalized this out-of-left-field proposal with the logic that he believed in "Canada First" – although how this would deal with Trump's complaints against Canada itself was left unsaid. Prime Minister Justin Trudeau, in turn, decided to make an impromptu visit to Mar-a-Lago and bring up the issue head-on with Trump himself. There, at an eleven-guest dinner, Trudeau voiced his concerns about the damage such tariffs would do to the Canadian economy. The reply he got from Trump was straightforward: if US tariffs are such a problem for Canada, perhaps the best thing would be for Canada to become the 51st state of the Union, with Trudeau changing his title of Prime Minister to that of governor – a response that did not go down well either with Trudeau or Canadian public opinion.[6]

Mexican President Claudia Sheinbaum took a very different approach. She responded with a public letter to Trump in which she laid out that Mexico was keen to work with the newly elected US administration, but that the announced US tariffs on Mexican imports bore no relation to the immigration and drug flows into the United States which her government was supposed to halt as a price for suspending the said tariffs. She was also firm in asserting that any such tariffs would elicit countervailing measures by Mexico, and, implicitly, the possibility of a trade war.[7] The available evidence would seem to indicate that, in the ensuing telephone conversation, Trump was much more accommodating to Mexico's demands than he had been to Canada's.[8]

Whatever happened to nearshoring and friendshoring?

As discussed in Chapter 4, a significant change that has taken place since 2016 has been the shift from a globalized world economy to a more fragmented one. Starting with the US-China trade and tech wars in 2018, and followed by the COVID-19 pandemic, the notion that the main criteria for investment and production decisions were strictly commercial was discarded, to be replaced by geopolitical and downright ideological notions. In this perspective, the rise of China and the ensuing US-China competition meant that trade and investment decisions from now on would be guided by where countries stood in this competition. The difficulties in securing masks, respirators, PPE and other equipment (mostly produced in China) during the pandemic led the US and European nations to embrace "nearshoring." This meant favoring availability over affordability, and prioritizing production facilities nearer the North Atlantic markets rather than in East Asia. This would presumably entail a more secure and prompt supply of masks in the event of a future pandemic, and the same would hold for other products.

This in turn would soon be followed by another neologism: "friendshoring." By this is meant the ideological proximity of governments to Western positions – the idea being that companies should invest in countries with governments sympathetic to the worldview dominating in Washington and Brussels. According to this rationale, as many US and European companies as possible should divest from their factories in China and move elsewhere, preferably closer to the US and European markets – something for which Latin America was ideally suited. Yet, world-class industries need world-class facilities and infrastructure to operate in, which China currently provides, but few Latin American countries do. This is why there has not been much "nearshoring" or "friendshoring" to the region. Perhaps the one exception to this is Mexico, the Latin American country with the most developed industrial sector, a solid infrastructure, a world-class role in the automotive parts sector, and a shared border with the United States. For the US, "nearshoring" doesn't get any closer than Mexico. Yet, none of this seems to have stood in the way of Trump's threats to impose a 25 percent tariff on Mexican goods entering the United States.

Unpredictability and exacerbated US-China competition

Mexico's predicament illustrates the difficulties of dealing with this volatile international environment, one that has become only more volatile with the election of Trump to a second term. Yet, there are certain pointers that can help us discern in which direction things will be going in years to come. The appointments of Senator Marco Rubio as Secretary of State and Representative Mike Waltz as National Security Advisor,[9] both *bona fide* China hawks (so much so that Rubio is currently subjected to China sanctions), would seem to show that, if anything, US-China relations, already on a downward slope, will get worse before they get better. Robert Lighthizer, who was the United States Trade Representative (USTR) in Trump's first term and who played a key role in the harsh China trade policy enacted at the time, will most likely be appointed to a senior position in the incoming administration, and his former chief of staff at the USTR, Jamieson Greer, has in fact been nominated as USTR.[10]

Yet, much as the Biden administration kept the tariffs imposed by Trump on China and otherwise embraced a strident anti-China line (one of the few areas of consensus among Democrats and Republicans in Washington), a second Trump term is likely to see some significant changes in China policy. A first item to be jettisoned is the framing of the US-China dispute as one between democracy and autocracy – a framing especially dear to President Biden, who promoted the three Democracy Summits held virtually in Washington in 2021, San Jose in 2023 and Seoul in 2024.[11] The same goes for the close work with allies in the G7 and NATO, which the Biden administration tried to leverage against China. This will be replaced by a unilateral approach, one that befits the "America First" motto.

The policy tools to be used will be tariffs along the lines discussed above (Trump has said that "tariff" is his favorite word in the English language); the banning of imports of various kinds of Chinese products; further banning of the sale of US high-tech products to China; and additional restrictions on Chinese investment projects in the US. Lighthizer has also indicated that the US should go for eliminating the World Trade Organization's Appellate Body – tasked with resolving international trade controversies, but now paralyzed due to the refusal of the US to approve the replacement of the judges whose term has expired.

The second Trump administration and the Global South

In another announcement via his social media platform, Truth Social, Trump warned the BRICS countries not to attempt to do anything to undermine the role of the US dollar as the dominant international currency, and that the penalties (again, in the form of high tariffs) for doing so would be severe.[12] This leads us to the question of the best approach to be followed by developing nations as they contend with the new administration in Washington DC and the role of ANA in it.

A first thing to keep in mind is that not all of Trump's foreign policy notions are necessarily destructive. His reluctance to pursue foreign military entanglements, so different from the liberal military interventionism of previous Republican (and Democratic) presidents, and his commitment to end the war in Ukraine, may provide a welcome respite in a world stretched to the limit by too many wars. For Latin America, a region that should recommit to one of its most prized assets, that of a Zone of Peace, this is especially significant. In the Middle East, the new administration will be torn between, on the one hand, the temptation to let Israel under Prime Minister Benjamin Netanyahu continue *sine die* with the wars in Gaza and Lebanon, and, on the other, the possibility of a grand bargain with Saudi Arabia, along the lines of the now inoperative Abraham Accords, that would bring peace to the region – the latter being incompatible with the former.

What should be obvious is that if there is one thing that will characterize US foreign policy in the second Trump administration it will be its unpredictability. This is something that the President-elect himself considers one of his greatest assets, both as a businessman and as a politician. In turn, given the background and record of his senior appointees in foreign policy and national security, the trade and tech wars with China are likely to escalate and be taken to another level. In this context, the pressure on developing nations – especially in Latin America, but also in Africa and Asia – to take sides will increase. And there will be some who will argue that there is no choice but to side with Washington this time around. The pressures will be too strong, and non-alignment will no longer be viable, or so the argument goes.

But to draw this conclusion from the winds that will blow in Washington in 2025–29 reflects a fundamental misunderstanding of the current structure of the international system and the nature of the dynamic of Great Power competition in our time. The latter depends significantly (though not exclusively) on the respective size of the economies of the competing Great Powers and their ability to deploy resources in this competition for the "hearts and minds" of the nations of the rest of the world. As discussed in this book, although the US economy is larger than China's, and in a variety of areas more advanced in science and technology, China's larger public sector and its capacity to allocate significant resources on critical projects abroad, as it has through the BRI, gives it an edge that compensates for the other advantages of the US in this regard. The degree to which the choice of ANA as the preferred foreign policy option is determined not by subjective preferences, or even by ideology, but by the very *structure* of the international system is illustrated by the case of Argentina under the presidency of Javier Milei.

A newcomer to politics, first-time Congressman and self-described "anarcho-capitalist," Milei ran for the Argentine presidency in 2023 denouncing China as a "communist dictatorship" from which he as President would stay away. While Argentine business would be welcome to continue to deal with Beijing, he said, his government would not do so. And, true to form, after taking office in the Casa Rosada in January 2024, Milei rejected an invitation to join the BRICS group and stated his commitment to a foreign policy guided by that of the United States and Israel, countries he visited repeatedly in the course of 2024. Yet, to the surprise of many, in October

2024 Milei announced his intention to visit Beijing in January 2025 for a scheduled meeting (later postponed) of the China-CELAC Ministerial Forum.[13] He has subsequently continued to heap praise on China as a trade and investment partner, one that does not impose conditions for doing business or making loans like other countries do.[14] What happened? What led to this extraordinary *volte face?*

The answer is straightforward. With a $286 billion foreign debt, Argentina has difficulties servicing it. A $5 billion swap loan provided by Beijing came due in June 2024, and the price for its renewal extracted by China was for Milei to stop his anti-China diatribes and announce a visit to China. This Milei proceeded to do. On other issues, like votes in multilateral organizations on the environment or on gender, the Milei government has continued with its highly idiosyncratic foreign policy, but when it comes to China there has been a 180-degree shift. This does not mean that Argentina has embraced ANA. Far from it. But it does mean that on what is perhaps the central international politics issue of our time, that of the US-China competition, Argentina under Milei will not automatically side with Washington but will evaluate pertinent issues on their merits and decide accordingly.

Yes, it is likely that the second Trump administration will take an even harsher line against China than it did in the first one. The problem is that, as far as the competition between Washington and Beijing for the "hearts and minds" of developing nations is concerned, while the United States can brandish plenty of sticks, it has few carrots at its disposal in what is essentially a competition at the socio-economic level. Being unable to grant additional market access, or to facilitate access to significant resources for infrastructure projects, Washington is, in a sense, fighting a boxing match with one hand tied behind its back.[15] In that regard, in terms of a foreign policy approach to dealing with the US-China competition, ANA will, if anything, gain *more* traction in years to come.

Relying on it may force the United States to come up with some genuine material incentives for developing nations to collaborate. Simply siding with Washington would remove the need for it to do so.

A light at the end of the tunnel?

Despite the considerable challenge a second Trump administration will entail for the Global South, there are some encouraging signs in this otherwise somber scenario. The signing of an EU-MERCOSUR trade agreement in Montevideo on December 5, 2024, after twenty-five years of negotiations, is one such positive signal. It is impossible to escape the conclusion that the signing was at least partly impelled by the results of the US presidential election held a month earlier.[16] At a time when the specter of protectionism is raising its ugly head not just in the United States, but elsewhere as well, the EU and the four member countries of MERCOSUR (Argentina, Brazil, Paraguay and Uruguay) reaffirmed their commitment to continue to liberalize international trade.[17] That they did so at a time when relations between the two largest members (Argentina and Brazil) are at an all-time low is testimony to their commitment to the larger issue of expanding trade and gaining greater market access for their economies. By dropping tariffs on 90 percent of goods in a market that would comprise a population of 700 million, an important step in the right direction has been taken. With the looming prospect of US tariffs, the EU is actively looking to diversify its markets, and this would be one of the largest trade agreements it has ever signed. None of this means that it is a done deal, as it still needs to be ratified by the EU member countries, where the agricultural lobby – particularly in France, but also in Poland and elsewhere – has resisted the deal with MERCOSUR for a quarter of a century. But it is a positive sign in an otherwise grim scenario in which Europe and Latin America were projected to be the two regions with the lowest growth in 2024. Both badly need to diversify their markets and give an additional impetus to their stagnating economies.

The agreement should also give a new lease on life to MERCOSUR, which has been in dire straits for some time, and may now recover at least some of the dynamism that elicited so much hope when it was first launched in 1991.

Notes

Preface

1. *Globely News*. (2024, May 23). Kenya's Ruto Balances the US and China.
2. Fortin, C. Heine, J. and Ominami, C. (2020). Latinoamérica: No Alineamiento y segunda Guerra Fría (Latin America: Non-Alignment and the Second Cold War). *Foreign Affairs Latinoamérica* 20:3; Fortin, C., Heine, J. and Ominami, C. (2023). European War and Global Pandemic: The Renewed Validity of Active Non-Alignment. *Global Policy*, January 30; Fortin, C., Heine, J. and Ominami, C. (eds.). (2023). *Latin American Foreign Policies in the New World Order: The Active Non-Alignment Option*. Anthem Press.
3. De la Torre, A., Didier, T., Ize, A., Lederman, D. and Schmukler, S. (2015). *Latin America and the Rising South: Changing World, Changing Priorities*. Washington D.C., The World Bank.
4. Hurun Global Rich List 2024. (2024). Hurun Research Institute.
5. Albert, M. (2024). *Navigating the Polycrisis: Managing the Futures of Capitalism and the Earth*. MIT Press.
6. Gramsci, A. (1971). *Selections from the Prison Notebooks*. International Publishers. See also, Babic, M. (2020). Let's Talk

about the Interregnum: Gramsci and the Crisis of the Liberal World Order. *International Affairs* 96:3, pp. 767–86.
7. Acharya, A. (2018). *The End of American World Order.* Polity.
8. Zakaria, F. (2012). *The Post-American World.* W. W. Norton.
9. Kassab, H. (2020). *Weak States as Spheres of Great Power Competition.* Routledge.

1 The War in Ukraine: Reactions from the Global South

1. Plokhy, S. (2023). *The Russia-Ukraine War: The Return of History.* W. W. Norton.
2. Ghervas, S. (2021). *Conquering Peace: From the Enlightenment to the European Union.* Harvard University Press.
3. Scholz, O. (2023, January–February). The Global Zeitenwende: How to Avoid a New Cold War in a Multipolar Era. *Foreign Affairs.*
4. *Reuters.* (2022, March 13). Sanctions Have Frozen Around $300 Bln, FinMin Says.
5. Arms Control Association. (2022). Ukraine, Nuclear Weapons and Security Assurances at a Glance: Fact Sheet and Brief.
6. Sarotte, M. E. (2022). *Not One Inch: America, Russia, and the Making of Post-Cold War Stalemate.* Yale University Press.
7. Serbin, A. (2022). Guerra en Ucrania y transición global: ¿Cómo se gestó y cómo nos afecta? (War in Ukraine and Global Transition: How Did It Originate and How Does It Affect Us?). *ERETE y CRIES.*
8. Lorenzini, M. E. (2022). La Política Exterior Argentina en la administración de Alberto Fernández: puntos de partida y posicionamiento frente a la invasión Rusia-Ucrania (Argentine Foreign Policy During the Alberto Fernandez Administration: Starting Points and Stance on the Russian invasion of Ukraine). *Anuario Mexicano de Asuntos Globales* 1:1.
9. *France 24.* (2022). Así reaccionaron los líderes de América Latina ante la invasión rusa de Ucrania (This is How Latin American Leaders Reacted to the Russian Invasion of Ukraine).

10. Sidiropoulos, E. and Gruzd, S. (2022, June). If You're Not Against Them, are You with Them? South Africa, Active Non-Alignment and the War in Ukraine. *TI Observer 21*.
11. Speech by the Minister of International Relations and Cooperation, Dr. Naledi Pandor, on the Occasion of the Budget Vote, DIRCO, May 12, 2022. Cited in Sidiropoulos and Gruzd (2022, June).
12. Cheng-Chwee, K. and Evans, P. (2022, June). ASEAN and Ukraine: Non-Alignment via Multi-Alignment? *TI Observer 21*.
13. Heine, J. (2023, March 8). Applying Active Non-Alignment for Ukraine Peace. *The Hindu*.
14. *The Economic Times*. (2023, August 15). India's Imports from Russia Doubled to USD 20.5 Billion in April–June Period.
15. Oppenheimer, A. (2023, February 23). La vergonzosa falta de apoyo de Argentina, Brasil, Colombia y México a Ucrania (The Embarrassing Lack of Support of Argentina, Brazil, Colombia and Mexico for Ukraine). *El Nuevo Herald*; Velasco, A. (2023, March 2). Latin America's Moral Failure, *Project Syndicate*.
16. *The Economic Times* (2022, 6 June).
17. Tokatlian, J. G. (2022, May 3). Ucrania: la guerra global (Ukraine: The Global War). *Clarín*.
18. PBS (2024, June 13). New $50 Billion Loan to Ukraine is Backed by Frozen Russian Assets. Here's How it Will Work.
19. *Reuters*. (2023, August 24). What is a BRICS Currency and is the US Dollar in Trouble?
20. Fortin, C., Heine, J. and Ominami, C. (eds.). (2023). *Latin American Foreign Policies in the New World Order: The Active Non-Alignment Option*. Anthem Press.
21. CEPAL. (2021). Perspectivas del Comercio Internacional de América Latina y El Caribe 2020: La Integración Regional es Clave Para la Recuperación de la Crisis (Perspectives on Latin America and the Caribbean's International Trade: Regional Integration is Key to Recover from the Crisis).
22. Heine, J. (2024, January 18). La odisea del cable al Asia-Pacifico (The Odyssey of the Cable to the Asia-Pacific). *La Tercera*.

23. *America Economia.* (2019, April 12). Ex Presidente en picada por lobby de Pompeo por liderazgo tecnologico chino (Former President Criticizes Pompeo Lobby on Chinese Tech Leadership).
24. Heine, La odisea del cable al Asia-Pacifico.
25. Gallagher, K. and Heine, J. (2021, January 26). Biden Needs to Reverse Trump's Economic Policy in Ecuador. *The Hill.*
26. Stuenkel, O. (2019, May 10). Huawei Heads South: The Battle over 5G Comes to Latin America. *Foreign Affairs.*
27. *Reuters.* (2010, October 12). Factbox. Soybean Oil Trade between Argentina and China.
28. Heine, J. (2020). Still Head Waiters Who are Occasionally Allowed to Sit? Heads of Mission after Covid-19. *The Hague Journal of Diplomacy* 20:4, pp. 648–58.
29. *La Tercera.* (2024, April 6). Embajador de China: Apoyar a las empresas chinas a operar y cooperar en Chile, así como proteger sus derechos, es una de mis principales responsabilidades (Chinese Ambassador: Supporting Chinese Companies to Operate and Cooperate in Chile, and Protecting Their Rights, is One of My Main Duties).
30. ECLAC. (2021). International Trade Outlook for Latin America and the Caribbean 2020: Regional Integration is Key to Post-Crisis Recovery.
31. World Bank. (2015). Latin America and the Rising South: Changing World, Changing Priorities.
32. Thucydides. (1972). *A History of the Peloponnesian War.* Penguin.
33. Hersh, S. (1984). *The Price of Power: Kissinger in the Nixon White House.* Summit Books.
34. Kassab, H. K. (2020). *Weak States as Spheres of Great Power Competition.* Routledge.
35. Stuenkel, O. (2020). *The BRICS and the Future of Global Order,* 2nd edition. Lexington Books; Economist Intelligence Unit. (2023). BRICS+ Impact: Plaudits and Brickbats; *The Economist.* (2023, August 17). The BRICS are Getting Together in South Africa.

36. Beattie, A. (2023, September 13). Global South is a Pernicious Term That Deserves to be Retired. *Financial Times*; Stewart, P. and Huggins, A. (2023, August 15). The Term "Global South" is Surging: It Should be Retired. Carnegie Endowment for International Peace.
37. Nye, J. (2023, November 1). What is the Global South? *Project Syndicate*; Heine, J. (2023, July 3). The Global South is on the Rise, But What Exactly is the Global South? *The Conversation*; Prashad. V. (2014). *The Poorer Nations: A Possible History of the Global South*. Verso; Braveboy-Wagner, J. (2003). *The Foreign Policies of the Global South: Rethinking Conceptual Frameworks*. Lynne Rienner.
38. *Financial Times*. (2023, October 18). Rush by West to Back Israel Erodes Developing Countries Support for Ukraine.

2 What is Active Non-Alignment and What Fuels It?

1. Application Instituting Proceedings in the name of the Republic of South Africa ("South Africa") against the State of Israel ("Israel"), International Court of Justice, December 29, 2023, https://www.icj-cij.org/case/192/institution-proceedings.
2. Application of the Prevention and Punishment of the Convention on the Crime of Genocide in the Gaza Strip ("South Africa vs Israel"), International Court of Justice, January 26, 2024, https://www.icj-cij.org/case/192/institution-proceedings.
3. *Al Jazeera*. (2023, December 5). Unpacking the Past: Mandela, the Keffiyeh and South Africa's Palestinian Embrace.
4. Tharoor, I. (2024, January 26). South Africa's Genocide Case Against Israel Spotlights a Global Divide. *The Washington Post*.
5. Wintour, P. (2024, April 6). The New World Disorder: How the Gaza War Disrupted International Relations. *The Guardian*.
6. *Al Jazeera*. (2024, April 7). Israel's War on Gaza: Six Months of Death and Destruction.
7. *Democracy Now*. (2024, March 13). UN: More Children Have Been Killed in Gaza Than in All Other Wars over Past Four Years.

8. B. Maddox, Director of Chatham House, cited by Wintour, P. (2024, April 6). The New World Disorder: How the Gaza War Disrupted International Relations. *The Guardian.*
9. Cited in Hogan, E. and Patrick, S. (2024, May 20). A Closer Look at the Global South. Carnegie Endowment for International Peace.
10. Deudney, D., Ikenberry, J. and Postel-Vinaym, K. (2023). *Debating Worlds: Contested Narratives of Global Modernity and World Order.* Oxford University Press.
11. Heine, J. (2024, February). The Global South, Gaza and the Rise of Active Non-Alignment. Blogpost. The Oxford Martin Program on Changing Global Orders.
12. *The New York Times.* (2024, March 31). Berlin Hardens Its Tone as Toll in Gaza Mounts.
13. *BBC News.* (2024, January 14). Namibia Criticizes German Support for Israel over ICJ Genocide Case.
14. Weizman, E. (2024, April 25). Three Genocides. *The London Review of Books* 46:8.
15. Kroenig, M. (2020). *The Return of Great Power Rivalry: Democracy Versus Autocracy from the Ancient World to the US and China.* Oxford University Press.
16. Heine, The Global South, Gaza and the Rise of Active Non-Alignment.
17. Spektor, M. (2023, May–June). In Defense of the Fence Sitters: What the West Gets Wrong about Hedging. *Foreign Affairs* 102:3.
18. Mishra, P. (2024, March 21). The Shoah after Gaza. *The London Review of Books* 46:6.
19. Acharya, A. (2018). *The End of American World Order.* Polity.
20. Albert, M. (2024). *Navigating the Polycrisis: Mapping the Futures of Capitalism and of the Earth.* MIT Press.
21. Osborn, C. (2022, December 20). Latin America and the New Non-Alignment. *Foreign Policy.*
22. Wolfers, A. (1965). *Discord and Collaboration: Essays on International Politics.* Johns Hopkins University Press.

23. Rubinstein, A. (1970). *Yugoslavia and the Non-Aligned World.* Princeton University Press.
24. Alam, M. (1977). The Concept of Non-Alignment: A Critical Analysis. *World Affairs* 166.
25. Menon, S. (2022, July 1). A New Cold War May Call for a Return to Non-Alignment. *Foreign Policy.*
26. Kassab, H. (2020). *Weak States as Spheres of Great Power Competition.* Routledge, p. 17.
27. Kassab, *Weak States,* p. 15.
28. Kuik, C-C. (2021). Getting Hedging Right: A Small State Perspective. *China International Strategy Review* 3.
29. Spektor, In Defense of the Fence Sitters.
30. Gash, T. G., Krastev, I. and Leonard, M. (2023, November 15). Living in an *À la Carte* World: What European Policymakers Should Learn from Global Public Opinion. European Council on Foreign Relations Policy Brief.
31. Doyle. M. (2023). *Cold Peace: Avoiding the New Cold War.* Liveright.
32. Wise, C. (2020). *Dragonomics: How Latin America is Maximizing (or Missing Out On) China's International Development Strategy.* Yale University Press.
33. Gallagher, K. (2016). *The China Triangle: Latin America's China Boom and the Fate of the Washington Consensus.* Oxford University Press.
34. Heine, J. and Rodrigues, T. (2023, Summer). Brazil is Ukraine's Best Bet for Peace. *Foreign Policy,* pp. 7–9.
35. *Financial Times.* (2023, May 11). China Deepens Ties in Latin America with Ecuador Free Trade Agreement.
36. Heine, J. (2023, October 30). Visita presidencial a Estados Unidos (Presidential Visit to the United States). *La Tercera.*
37. Ignatius, D. (2023, January 4). Biden's Unsentimental Foreign Policy Strategy. *The Washington Post.*
38. Toro, J. P. (2023, July 17). Las potencias extracontinentales en América Latina (Extraregional Powers in Latin America). *Política Exterior.*

39. Toro, Las potencias extracontinentales en América Latina.
40. Fernández de Soto, G. and Rugeles, A. (2023, July 17). América Latina-UE: Amor en Tiempos de Geopolítica (Latin America-EU: Love in Times of Geopolitics). *Política Exterior.*
41. Heine, J. (2023, July 16). Chile en la Cumbre UE-América Latina (Chile at the EU-Latin America Summit). *La Tercera.*
42. Unmussig, B. and Sitenko, A. (2021, April 15). *Divididos fracasamos: la diplomacia de las vacunas y sus implicaciones* (Divided We Fail: Vaccine Diplomacy and Its Implications). Heinrich Boll Foundation.
43. Voss, G., Zhou J. and Shuldner H. (2021, October 1). Vaccine Diplomacy in Latin America. *The Weekly Asado.* Latin American Program, The Wilson Center.
44. *Reuters.* (2024, June 14). Pentagon Ran Secret Anti-Vax Campaign to Undermine China During Pandemic.
45. Cooper, A. and Heine, J. (eds.). 2009. *Which Way Latin America? Hemispheric Politics Meets Globalization.* United Nations University Press.
46. Winter, B. (2022, February 24). Latin American Looks East. *Foreign Affairs.*

3 The Cold War, Decolonization and the Non-Aligned Movement

1. Rajak, S. (2014). No Bargaining Chips, No Spheres of Interest: The Yugoslav Origins of Cold War Non-Alignment. *Journal of Cold War Studies* 16:1, pp. 146–79.
2. However, the communiqué of an earlier meeting between Nehru and Tito refers to “the policy of non-alignment adopted and pursued by their respective countries.” Joint Statement by the President of the Federal People’s Republic of Yugoslavia and the Prime Minister of India 1954. Rajya Sabha Debates, December 22.
3. From a speech at the Opening of the Asian Relations Conference held in New Delhi in March–April 1947, *Selected Works of Jawaharlal Nehru,* Series II, Volume 2, http://www.claudearpi.net/wp-content/uploads/2016/12/SW02.pdf.

4. Nehru, J. (1985, January–March). Indian Foreign Policy. *India Quarterly*.
5. Nehru, J. (1949, May 4). No Departure from Past Pledges. *National Herald*.
6. Agreement between the Republic of India and the People's Republic of China on Trade and Intercourse between Tibet Region of China and India (1954).
7. Joint Statement of Prime Ministers of India and China (1954, June 28).
8. Životić, A and Čavoški, J. (2016, Fall). On the Road to Belgrade: Yugoslavia, Third World Neutrals, and the Evolution of Global Non-Alignment, 1954–1961. *Journal of Cold War Studies* 18:4.
9. Čavoški, J. (2010). Arming Non-alignment: Yugoslavia's Relations with Burma and the Cold War in Asia (1950–1955). Cold War International History Project Working Paper No. 61, Woodrow Wilson International Center for Scholars, April.
10. Rajak, No Bargaining Chips, No Spheres of Interest.
11. Nehru wrote in 1936: "Of course these movements [of passive resistance] exercised tremendous pressure on the British Government and shook the government machinery. But the real importance, to my mind, lay in the effect they had on our own people, and especially the village masses . . . Non-cooperation dragged them out of the mire and gave them self-respect and self-reliance . . . They acted courageously and did not submit so easily to unjust oppression." Nehru, J. (1958). Letter to Lord Lothian, January 17, 1936. In *A Bunch of Old Letters*. Asia Publishing House.
12. As the term "non-alignment" established itself in the international debate, reference to its active nature became standard in the pronouncements of the leaders of the movement: "Indonesia should not be a *passive* party in the area of international politics but . . . should be an *active* agent entitled to decide its own standpoint" (Sukarno, 1948). "Our policy is not merely negative or neutral or passive; it is a very active one . . . Non-alignment does not mean submission to what we consider evil. It is a positive and dynamic

approach to such problems that confront us" (Nehru, 1951, 1956). "The Non-Aligned Movement has become an effective weapon for the emancipation of new independent countries, the safeguarding of their independence and their active integration in international life as equitable members of the international community" (Tito, 1978). In the words of a Yugoslav student of the NAM: "as Nehru said in 1946, and as it was reaffirmed by the leaders of Burma, Indonesia, Yugoslavia and some other countries, non-alignment was an active policy, which in given situations required opting out or abstaining, but which always, whenever major world problems were at stake, called for an active position and initiative." Mates, L. (1972). *Non-Alignment Theory and Current Policy*. Belgrade and Oceana Publications.

13. A/RES/1236 (XII) (1957, December 14). Peaceful and Neighbourly Relations among States.
14. Government of India Ministry of External Affairs Report 1954–5.
15. Final Communique of the Asian African Conference, held at Bandung from April 18–24, 1955, https://bandungspirit.org/IMG/pdf/anri-bandung_conference-final_communique.pdf.
16. Summary of the Introductory Speeches at the Bandung Conference from April 18–19, 1955.
17. Opening Address of Sir John Kotelawala, Prime Minister of Ceylon, at the Asian-African Conference at Bandung, April 18, 1955.
18. Claudi, L. E. (2015, April). The Anti-Communist Third World: Carlos Romulo and the Other Bandung. *Southeast Asian Studies*.
19. Supplementary Speech by Zhou Enlai, the Chinese Premier, at the Opening of the Bandung Conference, April 18, 1955.
20. The principles are:
    a. Respect for fundamental human rights and for the purposes and principles of the Charter of the United Nations.
    b. Respect for the sovereignty and territorial integrity of all nations.
    c. Recognition of the equality of all races and of the equality of all nations large and small.

d. Abstention from intervention or interference in the internal affairs of another country.
e. Respect for the right of each nation to defend itself singly or collectively, in conformity with the Charter of the United Nations.
f. (a) Abstention from the use of arrangements of collective defense to serve the particular interests of any of the big powers.
   (b) Abstention by any country from exerting pressures on other countries.
g. Refraining from acts or threats of aggression or the use of force against the territorial integrity or political independence of any country.
h. Settlement of all international disputes by peaceful means, such as negotiation, conciliation, arbitration or judicial settlement as well as other peaceful means of the parties' own choice, in conformity with the Charter of the United Nations.
i. Promotion of mutual interests and cooperation.
j. Respect for justice and international obligations.

21. Životić and Čavoški, On the Road to Belgrade, 216.
22. Aburish, S. K. (2004). *Nasser, the Last Arab*. Thomas Dunne Books, St. Martin's Press.
23. Resolution 917 (XXXIV); Resolution A/RES/1785 (XVII).
24. Resolution A/ RES/3201 (S-VI).
25. Resolution A/RES/3281 (XXIX)
26. Lippmann, W. (1947.) *The Cold War: A Study in US Foreign Policy*. Harper and Brothers.
27. Pompeo, M. R. (2020, July 23). Communist China and the Free World's Future.
28. China Economic and Security Review Commission. (2023). Report to Congress.
29. Shu, C. (2019, May 20). Several Chip Companies Including Qualcomm and Intel Have Reportedly Stopped Supplying Huawei after Blacklist. *Techcrunch*.

30. Statements by the United States at the Meeting of the WTO Dispute Settlement Body (2023, January 27).
31. *The Guardian.* (2020, April 29). China Bristles at Australia's Call for Investigation Into Coronavirus Origin.
32. *The Washington Post.* (2023, October 29). China's Naval Provocations are Getting Too Blatant to Ignore.
33. China Economic and Security Review Commission. (2023).
34. Christensen, T. (2021, March 24). There Will Not be a New Cold War: The Limits of US-Chinese Competition. *Foreign Affairs.* For a refutation of Christensen's argument see Heine, J. (2023). A World Order in Crisis. In Fortin, C., Heine, J. and Ominami, C. (eds.). *Latin American Foreign Policies in the New World Order: The Active Non-Alignment Option.* Anthem Press.
35. Nye Jr., J. S. (2023, October). Not Destined for War. *Project Syndicate.*
36. Remarks by President Biden on the American Jobs Plan (2021, March 31).
37. Summit for Democracies Summary of Proceedings (2021, December 23).
38. Remarks by President Biden at the Summit for Democracy Opening Session (2021, December 9).
39. Foreign Ministry Spokesperson Wang Wenbin's Regular Press Conference (2023, March 15).
40. Kuo, K. (2021, June 15). Why the US Should Avoid Ideological Competition with China. *The China Project.*
41. WT/GC/W/773 (2019).

4 The Political Economy of Active Non-Alignment

1. Cardoso, F. H. and Faletto, E. (1979). *Dependency and Development in Latin America.* University of California Press (original Spanish edition published in 1969). Of the vast literature on dependency theory, this is the most emblematic text.
2. Williamson, J. (1990). *Latin American Adjustment: How Much Has Happened?* Institute for International Economics.

3. Ominami, C. (2017). *Clarooscuros de los Gobiernos Progresistas.* (Chiaroscuros of Progressive Governments). Catalonia.
4. ECLAC. (2023). Economic Study of Latin America and the Caribbean 2023 – Financing a Sustainable Transition: Investment to Grow and Confront Climate Change.
5. Michalet, C. (1985). *Le Capitalisme Mondial* (Global Capitalism). Presses Universitaires de France.
6. Fukuyama, F. (1992). *The End of History and the Last Man.* The Free Press.
7. Rodrik, D. (2022, May 9). A Better Globalization Might Rise from the Ashes of Hyper-Globalization. *Project Syndicate.*
8. Irwin, D. (2023). *The Return of Industrial Policy.* International Monetary Fund.
9. "Friendshoring" refers to the strategy of sourcing from geopolitically friendly countries, "nearshoring" to the outsourcing strategy by which a company transfers part of its production to nearby countries.
10. ECLAC, FAO, WFP. (2022). Towards Sustainable Food and Nutritional Security in Latin America and the Caribbean in Response to the Global Food Crisis.
11. Castillo, M. and Ominami, C. (forthcoming). Productive Transformation and New Industrial Policies in Latin America.
12. Prebisch, R. (1981). *Capitalismo Periférico: Crisis y Transformación* (Peripheral Capitalism: Crisis and Transformation). Fondo de Cultura Económica.
13. Komarkov, V. I. and Tomberg, R. G. (1979). *Economic Relations of the Soviet Union with Latin American Countries.* ECLAC, UNDP.
14. Frank, A. G. (1966) *The Development of Underdevelopment: The New Face of Capitalism.* Monthly Review Press.
15. Kennedy, J. F. (1961). Speech at the White House.
16. Ye, M. (2020). *The Belt and Road and Beyond: State-Mobilized Globalization in China 1998–2018.* Cambridge University Press.
17. OECD. (2014). *Making Innovation Policy Work.* OECD.

18. Rodrik D. (2017). *Straight Talk on Trade: Ideas for a Sane World Economy*. Princeton University Press; Stiglitz, J. (2020). *People, Power and Profits: Progressive Capitalism in an Age of Discontent*. W. W. Norton; Mazzucato, M. (2015). *The Entrepreneurial State: Debunking Public vs Private Sector Myths*. Public Affairs; Chang, H. J. (2015). *Economics: The User's Guide*. Bloomsbury.
19. Mazzucato, M. (2023). *Cambio Transformacional en America Latina y el Caribe: un enfoque de politica orientada por misiones* (Transformational Change in Latin America and the Caribbean: A Mission-Oriented Policy Approach). United Nations Economic Commission for Latin America and the Caribbean (ECLAC), January 2023, LC/TS. 2022/150/Rev1.
20. The inward growth model supported by import substitution was applied after the crisis of the 1930s.
21. Prebisch, *Capitalismo Periférico*; Pinto, A. (1959). *Chile, Un Caso de Desarrollo Frustrado*. Editorial Universitaria; Furtado, C. (1984). El Mito Del Desarrollo Económico (The Myth of Economic Development). Siglo XXI.
22. Fajnzylber, F. (1983). *La Industrialización Frustrada de América Latina* (Latin America's Frustrated Industrialization). Nueva Imagen.
23. United States Federal law that provides for extensive subsidies, particularly for the promotion of clean energy.
24. Agreement of the South American countries meeting in Brasília on May 30, 2023 at the initiative of President Lula da Silva.
25. Stein, B. (2013). *The Battle of Bretton Woods: John Maynard Keynes, Harry Dexter White, and the Creation of a New World Order*. Princeton University Press.
26. Galipolo, G. and Haddad, F. (2022, May). ¿Una moneda común para integrar a Sudamérica? (A Common Currency to Integrate Latin America?). *Nueva Sociedad*.

5 Active Non-Alignment and the ASEAN Way

1. Ayerbe, L. F. (2019). La Política de la Administración Trump Hacia América Latina: ¿Reinvención de la Doctrina Monroe?

(The Trump Administration's Policy Toward Latin America: Reinventing the Monroe Doctrine?). *Tempo do Mundo* 5:1.

2. Brands, H. (2023, December 3). America's Best Strategy for Cold War II is 200 Years Old. *Bloomberg.* For a Latin American perspective on the legacy of the Monroe Doctrine, see Morgenfeld, L. (2023). *Nuestra América frente a la doctrina Monroe* (Our America and the Monroe Doctrine). CLACSO.
3. Parameswaran, P. (2023, December 21). Southeast Asia and US-China Competition: Contours, Realities and Implications for the Indo-Pacific. The Wilson Center.
4. Kuik, C. and Evans, P. (2022). ASEAN and Ukraine: Non-Alignment via Multi-Alignment. *TI Observer 21.*
5. Mahbubani, K. and Sng, J. (2017). *The ASEAN Miracle: A Catalyst for Peace.* National University of Singapore Press.
6. Mahbubani, K. and Severino, R. (2014). *ASEAN: The Way Forward.* McKinsey and Company.
7. *Jakarta Globe.* (2023, August 8). ASEAN Poised to be Fourth Largest Economy in 2030.
8. Mahbubani, K. (2018, May 18). ASEAN: An Unexpected Success Story. *The Cairo Review of Global Affairs.*
9. Susanngkarn, C. (2010, June). The Chiang Mai Initiative Multilateralization: Origin, Development, Outlook. Asian Development Bank (ADB) Working Paper No. 230.
10. Acharya, A. (2017, August). The Myth of Asian Centrality? *Contemporary Southeast Asia* 39:2.
11. Tan, S. S. (2013). ASEAN Centrality. *CSCAP Regional Security Outlook 2013.* Council for Security Cooperation in the Asia Pacific.
12. Burges, S. (2018, May 3). UNASUR's Dangerous Decline: The Risks of a Growing Left-Right Split in South America. *Americas Quarterly.*
13. Rosales, O. (2023). Latin America, the COVID-19 Pandemic and the Restructuring of Value Chains. In Fortin, C., Heine, J. and Ominami, C. (eds.). *Latin American Foreign Policies in the New World Order: The Active Non-Alignment Option.* Anthem Press.

14. Acharya, The Myth of ASEAN Centrality?
15. Ward, R. (2020, November 25). RCEP Deal: A Geopolitical Win for China. International Institute for Strategic Studies.
16. Albertoni, N. and Heine, J. (2020, November 30). América Latina se está quedando al margen del mundo que viene (Latin America is Being Left Behind in the New and Upcoming World). *The New York Times.*
17. Babones, S. (2020, December 2). Cutting through the Hype on Asia's New Trade Deal. *Foreign Policy.*
18. Ye, Min. (2020). *The Belt and Road and Beyond: State-Mobilized Globalization in China: 1998–2018.* Cambridge University Press.
19. Chin, G. (2019, December 20). The Asian Investment and Infrastructure Bank – New Multilateralism: Early Development, Innovation and Future Agendas. *Global Policy.*
20. The White House. (2022, February). Indo-Pacific Strategy of the United States.
21. Medcalf, R. (2020). *Indo-Pacific Empire: America, China and the Struggle for the World's Pivotal Region.* Manchester University Press.
22. Wei, Z. (2022). The Evolution of the Quad: Driving Forces, Impacts and Prospects. *China International Strategy Review* 4.
23. Wicaksana, G. and Karim, M. (2023). How Regional Organization Survives: ASEAN, Hedging and International Society. *Contemporary Politics* 29:5.
24. Wicaksana and Karim, How Regional Organization Survives.
25. Lampton, D., Ho, S. and Kuik, C. (2020). *Rivers of Iron: Railroads and Chinese Power in Southeast Asia.* University of California Press.
26. *Nikkei Asia.* (2023, October 3). Indonesia's First High Speed Railway Opens: Five Things to Know.
27. *Reuters.* (2019, April 12). Malaysia, China Agree to Resume Train Deal after Slashing Cost.
28. Strangio, S. (2023, April 14). Laos-China Railway Launches Cross Border Service. *The Diplomat.*
29. The White House, Indo-Pacific Strategy of the United States.

30. *Times of India.* (2018, March 8). Quad Move Will Dissipate Like Sea Foam: China.
31. ASEAN. (2019, June 22). ASEAN Outlook on the Indo-Pacific. *ASEAN Portal,* https://asean.org.
32. Wicaksana and Karim, How Regional Organization Survives, p. 670.
33. US Department of State. (2021, August 4). US Support for the ASEAN Outlook on the Indo-Pacific. Office of the Spokesperson. Fact Sheet.
34. ASEAN. (2023). ASEAN-China Joint Statement on Mutually Beneficial Cooperation on ASEAN Outlook on the Indo-Pacific, https://asean.org.
35. Strangio, S. (2022, May 17). Assessing the Outcome of the US-ASEAN Special Summit. *The Diplomat.*
36. ASEAN. (2022). ASEAN-US Special Summit 2022. Vision Statement, https://asean.org.
37. *The Washington Post.* (2022, June 10). Biden's Hemispheric Summit of the Americas May End Up a Dud.
38. Kuik. C. (2023). Malaysian Conceptions of International Order: Paradoxes of Small-State Pragmatism. *International Affairs* 99:4, p. 1497.
39. Umar, A. (2023). The Rise of the Asian Middle Powers: Indonesian Conceptions of International Order. *International Affairs* 99:4.
40. Lee Hsien Loong (2020, July/August). The Endangered Asian Century: America, China and the Perils of Confrontation. *Foreign Affairs.*
41. Luong, D. (2024, January 9). Will Vietnam Get Caught in the Crosshairs of Great Power Politics Again? *Foreign Policy.*

6 From the Extreme West to Active Non-Alignment

1. *The Economist.* (2024, April 27). Dengue Disaster.
2. Brinck, S. (2021, September 30). Hecho en Chile: Vacunas con sello local (Made in Chile: Vaccines with a Local Imprint). Palabra Pública, Universidad de Chile.

3. Thornton, C. (2021). *Revolution in Development: Mexico and the Governance of the Global Economy.* University of California Press; Santa Cruz, H. (1984), *Cooperar o perecer? El dilema de la comunidad mundial* (Cooperate or Die? The Dilemma of the International Community). Grupo Editor Latinoamericano.
4. Long, T. (2015). *Latin America Confronts the United States: Asymmetry and Influence.* Cambridge University Press, pp. 25–73.
5. Khanna, P. (2019). *The Future is Asian: Commerce, Conflict and Culture in the 21st Century.* Simon and Schuster.
6. Group of Thirty. (2023, September). Why Does Latin America Underperform?
7. International Monetary Fund. (2024, April 19). Regional Economic Outlook: Western Hemisphere.
8. *Financial Times.* (2023, October 4). US Fears Mounting China Control of Peru's Infrastructure.
9. *Financial Times.* US Fears Mounting China Control of Peru's Infrastructure.
10. Braw, E. (2024, May 13). Peru Learns to Read the Fine Print in China Deals. *Foreign Policy.*
11. Kaplan. S. (2021). *Globalizing Patient Capital: The Political Economy of Chinese Finance in the Americas.* Cambridge University Press.
12. Ominami, C. (2019, August 9). Un no alineamiento activo (Towards Active Non-Alignment). *La Tercera.*
13. Fortin, C., Heine, J. and Ominami, C. (2020). Latinoamérica: no alineamiento y la segunda Guerra Fría (Latin America: Non-Alignment and the Second Cold War). *Foreign Affairs Latinoamérica* 20:3, pp. 107–15; Fortin, C., Heine, J. and Ominami, C. (2020, October). El no alineamiento activo: un camino para América Latina (Active Non-Alignment: The Way Forward for Latin America). *Nueva Sociedad*; Fortin, C., Heine, J. and Ominami, C. (eds.). (2023). *Latin American Foreign Policies in the New World Order: The Active Non-Alignment Option.* Anthem Press.
14. Fortin, C., Heine, J. and Ominami, C. (2023, January 31). European War and Global Pandemic: The Renewed Validity of

Active Non-Alignment. *Global Policy.* This and several of the following paragraphs draw on this piece.

15. Heine, J. (2006). Between a Rock and a Hard Place: Latin American Multilateralism after 9/11. In Newman, E., Thakur, R. and Tirman, J. (eds.). *Multilateralism Under Challenge? Power, International Order and Structural Change.* United Nations University Press.
16. Sanger, D. (2024). *New Cold Wars: China's Rise, Russia's Invasion and America's Struggle to Defend the West.* Crown.
17. Farrell, H. and Newman, A. (2023). *Underground Empire: How America Weaponized the World Economy.* Henry Holt.
18. *The New York Times.* (2022, May 8). Good News for Food, Bad News for War: Brazil Buys Russian Fertilizer.
19. Stuenkel, O. (2021, February 26). Latin American Governments are Caught in the Middle of the US-China Tech War. *Foreign Policy.*
20. Traub, J. (2022, July 9). Cold War 2.0 is Ushering in Non-Alignment 2.0. *Foreign Policy.*
21. *The New York Times.* (2022, December 31). Russia's War Could Make India's World.
22. Fortin, Heine and Ominami, European War and Global Pandemic.
23. Osborn, C. (2022, December 23). Latin America: The New Non-Alignment. *Foreign Policy.*
24. Government of Brazil. (2023, September 19). Speech by President Luiz Inácio Lula da Silva at the opening of the 78th UN General Assembly.
25. Heine, J. (2024, May 22). Kenyan President Will Receive White House Praise over Haiti Move, But Lack of Action across Americas Should Prompt Regional Soul-Searching. *The Conversation.*
26. Cepulani, G., Vigevani, T. and Schmitter, O. (2012). *Brazilian Foreign Policy in Changing Times: The Quest for Autonomy from Sarney to Lula.* Lexington Books.

27. Amorim, C. (2023). Brazil and the Global South. In Fortin, Heine and Ominami (eds.). *Latin American Foreign Policies in the New World Order*, pp. 251–62.
28. Heine, J. and Rodrigues, T. (2023, Summer). Brazil is Ukraine's Best Bet for Peace. *Foreign Policy*, pp. 7–9.
29. *CEBRI Journal* 3:9. (2024, January–March). Special issue on the first year Lula's foreign policy.

7 The Global South and Active Non-Alignment

1. Cooper, A. and Thakur, R. (2012). *Group of Twenty*. Routledge.
2. Tripathi, S. (2020). *India's Foreign Policy: Dilemma over Non-Alignment 2.0.* Sage.
3. United Nations. (2023, September 4). Secretary-General's Opening Remarks at Press Conference, New Delhi.
4. G20. (2023). One Earth, One Family, One Future: G20 New Delhi Leader's Declaration.
5. BFMTV. (2023, October 27). Face-to-Face Interview with Dominique de Villepin, https://www.youtube.com/watch?v=EreEL6lCyek.
6. Oglesby, C. (1969). Vietnamism Has Failed . . . The Revolution Can Only be Mauled, Not Defeated. *Commonweal* 90.
7. Heine, J. (2023, July 3). The Global South is on the Rise, But What Exactly is the Global South? *The Conversation*.
8. Stewart, P. and Higgins, A. (2023, August 15). The Term "Global South" is Surging: It Should be Retired. Carnegie Endowment for International Peace; Nye, J. (2023, November 1). What is the Global South? *Project Syndicate*; Mohan, R. (2023, December 9). Is There Such a Thing as the Global South? *Foreign Policy.*
9. United Nations Development Program. (2004, December 19). Forging a Global South: United Nations Day for South-South Cooperation.
10. Beattie, A. (2023, December 14). The Global South is a Pernicious Term That Should be Retired. *Financial Times.*
11. Shidore, S. (2023, August 31). The Return of the Global South. *Foreign Affairs.*

12. *Aljazeera*. (2023, September 16). Global South Leaders Demand End of "Plundering International Order."
13. Hogan, E. and Patrick, S. (2024, May 20). A Closer Look at the Global South. Carnegie Endowment for International Peace.
14. UNCTAD. (2023). Key Statistics and Trends in International Trade 2022, p. 10.
15. World Trade Organization. (2022). WTO Seminar Looks at How South-South, Multiparty Cooperation Supports Developing Economies.
16. UNCTAD. (2023). World Investment Report 2022, Annex 2, p. 199.
17. Joint Leaders Statement (2022, May 24). Quadrilateral Security Dialogue.
18. Lieberherr, B. (2023, February). The "Rules-Based Order": Conflicting Understandings. *CSS Analyses in Security Policy* 317.
19. *Financial Times*. (2023, April 20). Is There Such a Thing as a Rules-Based International Order? The Rachman Review. Transcript of podcast with John Ikenberry.
20. Lieberherr, The "Rules-Based Order."
21. For background, see Stuenkel, O. (2020). *The BRICS and the Future of Global Order*. 2nd edition. Lexington Books.
22. Cooper, A. (2016). *The BRICS: A Very Short Introduction*. Oxford University Press.
23. Wolf, M. (2012, March 30). Does the BRICS Group Matter? Council on Foreign Relations.
24. Wolf, Does the BRICS Group Matter?
25. Economist Intelligence Unit. (2023). BRICS+ Impact: Plaudits and Brickbats.
26. Pant, H. (2023). From BRICS to BRICS+: Old Partners and New Stakeholders. Special Report No. 214. Observer Research Foundation.
27. Stuenkel, O. (2014). *IBSA: The Rise of the Global South*. Routledge.
28. *Xinhua*. (2023, July 26). China Will Always be a Member of the "Global South" Says Wang Yi.

29. Leonard A. (2006, September 16). No Consensus on Beijing Consensus. Neoliberalism with Chinese Characteristics? Or the Long-Lost Third Way? *Salon.*
30. Brautigam, D. and Rithmire, M. (2021, February 6). The Chinese "Debt Trap" is a Myth. *The Atlantic*; Brautigam D. and Zhang H. (2013). Green Dreams: Myth and Reality in China's Agricultural Investment in Africa. *Third World Quarterly* 34:9, pp. 1676–96.
31. *The Indian Express.* (2023, February 20). India against China-Led Investment Facilitation Proposal at WTO: Official; see also World Trade Organization. (2021, February 19). The Legal Status of "Joint Statement Initiatives" and their Negotiated Outcomes. Communication of India and South Africa, Doc. WY/GC/W/819.
32. International Centre for Settlement of Investment Disputes. Comments on the Proposed Amendments to the ICSID Rules Submitted by China, https://icsid.worldbank.org/sites/default/files/amendments/state-input/China Comments 12.28.18.pdf.
33. United Nations Human Rights Office of the High Commissioner. (2022, August 31). Assessment of Human Rights Concerns of the Xinjiang Uyghur Autonomous Region, People's Republic of China.
34. Permanent Mission of the People's Republic of China to the United Nations Office in Geneva. (2022). Remarks of the Chinese Mission Spokesperson Liu Yuyin on the News Release by Certain Special Procedural Mandate Holders.
35. Permanent Mission of the People's Republic of China to the United Nations Office in Geneva. (2022, September 26). Joint Statement Delivered by Pakistan on Behalf of Group of Countries at the 51st Session of the Human Rights Council.
36. International Federation of Human Rights. (2023). UN Human Rights Council Voted against Debate on Human Rights Violations in China's Xinjiang Region, http://www.fidh.org/en/region/asia/china-human-rights-council-voted-against-a-debate-on-human-rights.

37. Ominami, C. (2024, January 23). Le Sud global peut agir comme constructeur d'un ordre international plus équilibré (The Global South Can Contribute to the Building of a More Balanced International Order). *Le Monde.*

Conclusion

1. Sagoo, R. and Dias, T. (2024, May 21). The ICC Prosecutor's Application for Arrest Warrants Explained. Chatham House.
2. *CNN.* (2024, May 20). Biden Denounces ICC for "Outrageous" Implication of Equivalence between Israel and Hamas.
3. *The Hill.* (2024, May 20). Republicans Renew Call for Sanctions on ICC Following Netanyahu Arrest Warrant.
4. *BBC News.* (2024, May 21). US Signals Support for Possible ICC Sanctions over Israel Warrants.
5. *The Guardian.* (2020, September 7). US Imposes Sanctions on Top International Criminal Court Officials.
6. Roth, K. (2024, May 7). Biden Should Not Stand in the Way of the ICC. *Foreign Policy.*
7. *MSNBC.* (2024, March 14). More Children Killed in Gaza in Four Months Than in Four Years of War: Report.
8. Mulder, N. (2022). *The Economic Weapon: The Rise of Sanctions as a Tool of Modern War.* Yale University Press.
9. Farrell, H. and Newman, A. (2023). *Underground Empire: How America Weaponized the World Economy.* Henry Holt and Company, p. 13.
10. Jackson, V. (2024). *Grand Strategies of the Left: The Foreign Policy of Progressive Worldmaking.* Cambridge University Press, p. 120.
11. Center for Economic and Policy Research. (2023, May 4). New Report Finds That Economic Sanctions are Often Deadly and Harm People's Standard of Living in Target Countries.
12. *ABC News.* (2024, August 14). Trump Campaign Faces Backlash after Posting Two Images That Disparage Immigrants. They Read: Import the Third World. Become the Third World.

13. Cohen, R. (2022, December 31). Russia's War Could Make it India's World. *The New York Times.*
14. Albert, M. (2024). *Navigating the Polycrisis: Mapping the Futures of Capitalism and of the Earth.* MIT Press.
15. Allison, G. (2017). *Destined for War: Can America and China Avoid the Thucydides Trap?* Scribe.
16. Heine, J. (2024, July 12). SA Embraces Active Non-Alignment, a Foreign Policy for Our Time. *Business Day.*
17. Vanden Heuvel, K. (2022, January 5). What a Sensible Ukraine Policy Should Look Like. *The Washington Post.*
18. Guterres, A. (2024, February 7). Secretary-General's Remarks to the General Assembly on Priorities for 2024. United Nations.
19. Long, Tom. (2022). *A Small State's Guide to Influence in World Politics.* Oxford University Press.
20. Cook, S. (2019, April 26). Loving Dictators is as American as Apple Pie. *Foreign Policy.*
21. Kassab, H. (2020). *Weak States as Spheres of Influence of Great Power Competition.* Routledge.
22. *The Washington Post.* (2024, May 21). As US Influence in Africa Wanes, Kenya Bucks the Trend.
23. Heine, J. and Rodrigues, T. (2023, Summer). Brazil is Ukraine's Best Bet for Peace. *Foreign Policy,* pp. 7–9.
24. *Foreign Policy.* (2024, Spring). The India Issue; see also Tripathi, S. (2020). *India's Foreign Policy: Dilemma over Non-Alignment 2.0.* Sage.
25. Heine, J. (2024, August 5). In "Bamboo Diplomacy" Late Vietnam Leader Nguyen Phu Trong Left a Path for Smaller Nations to Navigate Great Power Rivalries. *The Conversation.*
26. Heintz, S. (2024). A Logic for the Future: International Relations in an Age of Turbulence. Rockefeller Brothers Fund.
27. Stuenkel, O. (2016). *Post-Western World: How Emerging Powers are Remaking Global Order.* Polity.
28. Puri, S. (2024). *Westlessness: The Great Global Rebalancing.* Hachette.

29. Jacobs. M, Lent, A. and Watkins, K. (2003). *Progressive Globalisation: Towards an International Social Democracy.* Fabian Ideas 608.
30. Gowan, R. (2024, June 12). Peace and Security: Redefining the UN's Prime Purpose. *SDG Action.* HLPF edition.
31. *Financial Times.* (2024, August 21). The US-Backed Railway Sparking a Battle for African Copper.
32. Boston University Global Development Policy Center. (2024). Chinese Loans to Africa Database, https://www.bu.edu/gdp/chinese-loans-to-africa-database.
33. *Financial Times.* The US-Backed Railway.
34. *Financial Times.* The US-Backed Railway.

Afterword

1. Bremmer, I. (2024, November 12). What Trump's Return Means for the World. *Project Syndicate.*
2. *Financial Times.* (2024, November 26). Donald Trump Says He Will Hit China, Canada and Mexico with New Tariffs.
3. *Newsweek.* (2024, December 1). Republican Strategist Calls Donald Trump's Bluff on Tariffs.
4. The December 2018 arrest and subsequent detention for almost three years of Meng Wanzhou – a vice-president (and daughter of the company founder) of Huawei, China's leading telecommunications company, and at the time in transit at Vancouver International Airport – at the request of the US government, on questionable legal grounds, sent Canada-China relations on a downward spiral from which they have not recovered to this day. See Keitner, C. (2019, January 25). Trump, Huawei and the Politics of Extradition. *Foreign Affairs.*
5. *El Dictamen.* (2024, November 26). Canadian Opposition Leader is Willing to Exclude Mexico from USMCA.
6. *Globe & Mail.* (2024, December 3). Canada Could be "51st state" Trump Joked During Mar-a-Lago Dinner with Trudeau.
7. *The New York Times.* (2024, November 26). Mexican President Raises Possibility of Retaliatory Tariffs on US Goods.

8. *The Washington Post.* (2024, November 28). Mexican President Has “Excellent” Talk with Trump, Dismisses Tariff Threat.
9. Drezner, D. (2024, December 8). The Evolution of Marco Rubio. *The New York Times.*
10. Lighthizer, R. (2024, November 1). Donald Trump’s Remedies Reflect America’s Troubled Reality. *Financial Times.* See also his book *No Trade is Free: Changing Course, Taking on China, and Helping America’s Workers.* HarperCollins, 2024. For a wide-ranging review of Lighthizer’s book and the issues he raises, see Kuttner, R. (2024, December 19). The Import of Exports. *The New York Review of Books* 71:20.
11. Diamond, L. (2024, November 8). Democracy without America? What Trump Means for Global Democratic Momentum. *Foreign Affairs.*
12. *The Guardian.* (2024, December 1). Trump Threat of 100% Tariffs against BRICS Countries Raises Trade War Fears.
13. Heine, J. (2024). Active Non-Alignment and Great Power Competition in Our Time. *Asuntos Globales* 1:1.
14. *The Economist.* (2024, November 28). An Interview with Javier Milei, Argentina’s President.
15. Porter, E. (2024, November 26). Trump Can’t Bully the World Out of Doing Business with China. *The Washington Post.*
16. *Financial Times.* (2024, December 6). EU Strikes Blockbuster Trade Deal with MERCOSUR.
17. *The New York Times.* (2024, December 7). As Trump Threatens Tariffs, Europe and South America Strengthen Ties. See also Beattie A. (2024, December 9). The Mercosaurus Roars. *Financial Times.*

Index